More praise for

Of The People, By The People:
The case for a participatory economy

"*I read Participatory Economics with absolute fascination. Some leading activist scholars have moved towards a more explicit consideration of post-capitalist alternatives. Lucid, thorough, and iconoclastic, Participatory Economics is an outstanding contribution to this important genre of radical social theory.*"

--*Andrej Grubacic*

Andrej Grubacic is Associate Professor and Department Chair of the Anthropology and Social Change program at the California Institute of Integral Studies. He is an outspoken protagonist for "new anarchism," and co-author with Staughton Lynd of Wobblies and Zapatistas (PM Press 2008).

"*Participatory Economics is a vision, a practice and, for Robin Hahnel, a particular model. As a vision, it points to a new society in which people can develop as free and associated producers outside of the domination of their own product (capital) or of a state which stands over and above them. As a practice, it is embodied in the collective struggles for cooperation rather than competition that have occurred for centuries and which are reflected today in processes of participatory budgeting and the development of worker cooperatives. And, as the model advanced by Hahnel, it is a powerful demonstration both of the theoretical feasibility of participatory economics as well as of the flaws and inherent bias of mainstream economics as taught in universities and promoted in the capitalist mass media.*"

-- Michael Lebowitz

Michael Lebowitz is professor emeritus of economics at Simon Faser University in Vancouver Canada, and author of Build It Now: Socialism for the Twenty-First Century (Monthly Review 2006). He was Director, Program in Transformative Practice and Human Development, Centro Internacional Miranda, in Caracas, Venezuela, from 2006 to 2011.

DEDICATION

To my grandchildren, Eleanor and Beckett, and to all who Occupy -- past and future.

ACKNOWLEDGEMENTS

I would like to thank Meredith Jordan for help with copy editing and Yotam Marom who helped plan this book and provided valuable suggestions and feedback. In the end, Marom was unable to participate as co-author because working as an activist and organizer for Occupy Wall Street and the Organization for a Free Society became an urgent priority.

OF THE PEOPLE, BY THE PEOPLE

The case for a participatory economy

Robin Hahnel

This edition first published by Soapbox 2012
©Robin Hahnel 2012

www.soapboxpress.org

Distributed by AK Press

www.akpress.org

ISBN: 978-0-9830597-6-9

Cover design by Jordan Karr-Morse

CONTENTS

CHAPTER ONE

INTRODUCTION

About This Book

This book is for people who want to know what a desirable alternative to capitalism might look like. It is for people who want more than rosy rhetoric and Pollyannaish descriptions of people working in harmony. It is for people who want to dig into what economic justice and economic democracy mean. It is a book for optimists—who believe the human species must be capable of something better than succumbing to competition and greed or authoritarianism, and would like to know how we can do it. It is also a book for skeptics—who demand to be shown, explicitly and concretely, how a modern economy can dispense with markets and authoritarian planning, and how hundreds of millions of people can manage their own division of labor efficiently and equitably.

This book is written by someone who understands that capitalism will not disappear overnight – falling victim to some mythical internal contradiction. It is written by someone who understands that capitalism can only be replaced by a better economic system when a majority is ready to do so. And it is written by someone who knows this will only occur after many progressive mass movements have waged many successful struggles over many years, and after millions of people have created a multitude of real world experiments in different forms of equitable cooperation even while global capitalism persists. It is written by someone who appreciates the Occupy Wall Street movement as an important new beginning where he lives, here in the United States, but understands that we are still far from capitalism's "end game."

This book is also written by someone who understands that not all versions of capitalism are equally terrible. In what are often called "social democratic" versions of capitalism, financial institutions can be competently regulated, investment priorities can be guided by some political planning, environmental, health, and safety regulations can be enforced, workers can be represented by unions who bargain successfully for better wages, and people's health, education, and retirement needs can be provided for through adequately funded public programs. On the other hand, in what are now called "neoliberal" versions of capitalism, giant corporations, and rapacious financial institutions in particular, reign supreme, unregulated markets compel socially irrational uses of our productive resources and energies, economic crises are more frequent and severe, the environment is dangerously stressed, starved of resources, public services deteriorate, and the distribution of income and wealth becomes ever more unequal. Anyone who cannot see that social democratic capitalism is preferable to neoliberal capitalism is simply not paying attention.

But while fighting for progressive reforms makes sense as long as capitalism persists, stopping short of replacing capitalism with a new economic system in the twenty-first century makes no sense for three reasons.

- •While social democratic capitalism is *less* unfair, *less* insecure, *less* inefficient, and treads *less* heavily on the environment than neoliberal capitalism, social democratic capitalism cannot provide full economic justice and democracy. It cannot tap the economic creativity and potentials of the entire population. It cannot fully and adequately protect an environment that is seriously at risk.

In short, social democratic capitalism is not good enough. We can, and must do much better.

- As long as productive resources are privately owned and decisions are guided by market forces(as they continue to be under social democratic capitalism)those fighting for reforms to make the system more secure, equitable, efficient, and sustainable are destined to swim upstream against the destructive currents unleashed by the private enterprise market system. Why should we accept this handicap? Why should we concede our opponents more money and a louder media megaphone in every struggle?

- As long as the defining institutions of capitalism are left in place – that is as long as what the great American social democratic leader, Michael Harrington, called the "grand social democratic compromise" allows them to be -- any gains progressives win are always at risk of being rolled back. The history of the last thirty years is a painful object lesson. During the middle third of the twentieth century reformers made headway in many of the advanced capitalist countries. And to be honest, many of us born in the aftermath of the Great Depression came to view this kind of progress as inevitable, even if frustratingly slow and incomplete. But during the last thirty years giant corporations launched a free market ideological counter attack rolling back one successful reform after another. Today, whether it be Greece, Portugal, Spain, Ireland, Italy, the UK, Canada, or the U.S., prudent regulations have been abandoned and social safety nets are being torn asunder;

why? Because the top 1% has the *chutzpah* to use a crisis their neoliberal policies helped create to continue to prosper at the expense of the bottom 99% in one advanced capitalist country after another. Failing to disarm a defeated enemy is not in the field manuals good generals follow, which is what leaving the private enterprise market system in place amounts to.

There is much to be said about building bigger and more powerful progressive movements, as well as about strategy and tactics for how best to protect ourselves and the environment until we can replace capitalism. When we have built a majoritarian movement ready to launch a new economic system worthy of the twenty-first century, there will be much to say about how to dispatch capitalism into the dustbin of history in the most expeditious way. But while these issues are discussed briefly in the last chapter, the purpose of this short book is to spell out concretely what a desirable alternative to capitalism might look like.

Auntie TINA

"[Capitalism] is not a success. It is not intelligent, it is not beautiful, it is not just, it is not virtuous -- and it doesn't deliver the goods. In short, we dislike it, and we are beginning to despise it. But when we wonder what to put in its place, we are extremely perplexed." -- John Maynard Keynes

With all the work we must do responding to crises and protecting people and the environment, why is it important to take the time to think through how a desirable alternative to capitalism can work?

There is no shortage of scathing indictments of capitalism, and serious anti-capitalist movements have been around since capitalism first burst on history's stage. Yet capitalism has survived despite its many flaws. Why is it so hard to get rid of this bad penny?

The people who profit most from capitalism have developed an arsenal of weapons to disempower the rest of us. There are bright lights flickering in Times Square, clever consumer goods to buy us off, the alluring myth that we are all middle class, as well as the contradictory myth that anyone willing to work hard can climb up the class hierarchy. There are various social cleavages which pit us against one another, a sophisticated corporate media that lulls us into a stupor, and the illusion of democracy because we are free to buy and vote as we please. Ultimately there is the violence of the police and military if we step too far out of line—or simply come from a more threatened community. Together, all this forms a brutally efficient system of domination that protects the privileges of the few at the expense of the many.

But this is not the only reason capitalism has been with us this long. While capitalism is incompatible with the best of human potentials it is compatible with some of our worst potentials. No economic system totally at odds with human nature could possibly survive as long as capitalism already has if it did not resonate with some part of what human beings can become. Defenders of capitalism play on this fact by claiming that humans can *only* be reliably motivated by greed and fear, that most people are *incapable* of making good economic decisions and therefore must be told what to do by others, and therefore we can only hope that placing most under the command of a few, and forcing the greedy and fearful to compete against one another in markets will yield reasonably desirable outcomes. This is the time honored "human nature" defense of capitalism. What it amounts to is the defense of a sorry-assed economic system as our destiny because we are a sorry-assed species.

The fallacy in this argument is simple: It fails to acknowledge that humans have other potentials as well – potentials that cannot be fulfilled under capitalism but can become the basis for an economic system in which people manage their own economic activities democratically, fairly, sustainably, and efficiently. The fallacy in the "human nature" defense of capitalism is not that people are not capable of acting out of greed and fear and obeying orders, because in a hierarchical system that rewards greedy and fearful behavior many of us will often behave in these ways. The fallacy is in asserting that in a system where people are given the opportunity to make their own decisions, where people are positively rewarded for embracing a fair distribution of the burdens and benefits of economic activity, where people are rewarded for acting in solidarity with others, that we are incapable of doing so. The fact that we can see people behaving in these positive ways every day despite disincentives to do so is clear evidence that such behavior is not beyond human nature.

This "the ugly side of human nature is all there is to human nature" lie is the launching pad for the TINA defense of capitalism. In the early 1980s Margaret Thatcher turned a rejoinder long used by self-serving ruling elites whenever their victims begin to grumble -- "There Is No Alternative" -- into an unforgettable acronym, TINA. Last century many on the left responded to the TINA defense of capitalism by pointing to the Soviet Union, or Maoist China, or some other Communist country. Others who could not ignore the increasingly obvious deficiencies in Communist societies succumbed to TINA and resigned themselves to trying to make capitalism a little more humane. Both responses were mistakes. Communism was never a desirable alternative to capitalism, and therefore never a compelling response to TINA. On the other hand, TINA is nothing more than a desperate assertion made by those who are hard pressed to defend capitalism on its merits.

This short book describes a feasible alternative to capitalism in which workers manage themselves instead of working for an employer or a commissar, and worker and consumer councils plan their own interrelated activities themselves—

without recourse to either central planners or markets. It explains how this "participatory economy" can work efficiently and fairly; why it need not tie us up in endless debates in interminable meetings; why it will motivate people to work hard and enterprises to innovate; and why it will protect the natural environment better than any economic system before it. This book is an answer to any, who like Lord Keynes, are increasingly disgusted with capitalism but find themselves "perplexed about what to put in its place." What follows demonstrates that TINA is not only an empty assertion, it is the ultimate "big lie." There *is* a highly desirable alternative to capitalism that builds on the best (rather than the worst)of human potentials, and it is perfectly feasible.

We need a compelling response to TINA because without a vision of something worth fighting for we cannot expect people to take the risks necessary to change things. We need a response to TINA because without a clear idea of where we want to go we cannot forge a strategy for how to get from here to there. Finally, we need a response to TINA because you can't beat something with nothing.

CHAPTER TWO

PARTICIPATORY ECONOMICS: ORIGINS

Will the twenty-first century be a century when an increasingly educated global population insists on fully participating in making all the economic decisions that affect our lives? A century when all forms of economic injustice will be seen for what they are and no longer tolerated? A century when humans fully embrace our role as stewards rather than exploiters of the natural environment? A century when we finally throw off all shackles to achieve our full potential as human beings? If so, the twenty-first century will be a century that embraces some kind of "participatory economics."

"Participatory economics" is an economic vision that has been shared by many over the past two hundred years. It is a vision of people managing their own economic affairs democratically and equitably instead of being driven by greed and fear to compete against one another.

"Participatory economics" is also a theoretical model first elaborated in the early 1990s that spells out how all the different kinds of economic decisions that must be made in any economy could be made in new and different ways.[1] This

1 Michael Albert and Robin Hahnel, *The Political Economy of Participatory Economics*. (Princeton University Press, 1991), "Socialism As It Was Always Meant to Be," *Review of Radical Political Economics (24, 3&4)*, Fall and Winter 1992: 46-66, and "Participatory Planning," *Science & Society (56, 1)*, Spring 1992: 39-59.

model established for the first time that the kind of economy long envisioned by many who were disgusted by the economics of competition and greed was theoretically possible. It also disproved a version of TINA expressed by a prominent British economist, Alec Nove, in the early 1980s, who wrote: "In a complex industrial economy the interrelation between its parts can be based in principle either on freely chosen negotiated contracts [i.e., markets], or on a system of binding instructions from planning offices [i.e. central planning]. *There is no third way.*"[2]

Participatory economics has been applied in the past with considerable success, for example by tens of millions of workers and peasants inspired by anarchist teachings during the Spanish Civil War. But we do not have to look only to the past to see participatory economics in practice. People in Vancouver, Atlanta, Chicago, London, Helsinki, Barcelona, Athens, New Delhi, and Sydney have organized to study the model of participatory economics described in this book and bring it to the attention of other activists. There are people self-consciously attempting to practice participatory economics principles in collectives in a number of countries. In places like Porto Allegre, Brazil, and communal councils and municipal assemblies in cities and towns all over Venezuela, something similar to the kind of participatory planning that is a key part of the model presented in this book is being practiced under the name of "participatory budgeting." "Solidarity economics" has already become a major force in many countries in Latin America. Progressive forces in North America and Europe are busy creating what we call "the new economy" to replace the economics of competition and greed as it increasingly fails to meet even our most basic needs.

But "participatory economics" should be understood for what it is: an alternative vision that dates back to the birth of capitalism, now backed by a formal model demonstrating that

2   Alec Nove, *The Economics of Feasible Socialism*. (George Allen & Unwin, 1983): 44.

this vision is feasible in theory, and a growing number of initiatives proving that popular economic decision making does work. A participatory economy has yet to be put into practice fully on a large scale, and still has a long way to go before all of the kinks are worked out. It is offered here as a work in progress and the beginning of a conversation you can take part in.

CHAPTER THREE

ECONOMIC BASICS

What Is an Economy?

An economy is simply a system for organizing production and consumption of goods and services and the disposal of wastes. Assuming that every person is not entirely self-sufficient, an economic system must coordinate what amounts to a division of labor in which people produce different things and everyone consumes things made by others. It's a collection of institutions that govern what we make, how we make it, who gets how much, and where it goes when it's broken or unwanted.

Any economy has to provide answers to a few basic questions: Who will do what tasks? How are people compensated for what they do? How will we choose among alternative ways of making things? How will productive resources, including different kinds of labor, be allocated among enterprises? How will the final goods and services produced be distributed among consumers? In sum, every economy decides how to distribute the burdens and benefits of social economic activity among those who participate in the economy.

For example, capitalism is a system in which production is organized and carried out in enterprises owned by stockholders who demand that their corporations maximize their profits. Productive resources are privately owned, and who gets to use different resources, categories of labor, and produced goods and services is decided through market exchanges. Those who own shares of stock and resources need do no work. A minority of employees do the empowering and relatively pleasant tasks of organizing and directing the work process, while all the dangerous, tiring, boring tasks are done by everyone else. People are compensated based on how much productive property they own (or don't own), and on how much bargaining power they have (or don't have) in the labor market. In capitalism those who own the productive resources appropriate the lion's share of the benefits of social economic activity while shouldering few of the burdens; managers and professionals are relatively well rewarded for performing most of the empowering and desirable tasks; and ordinary workers do most of the undesirable tasks while receiving much less economic benefits. Sound familiar?

On the other hand, in a participatory economy, production is organized and carried out in worker councils where each member has one vote. By participating in a planning procedure, worker councils receive permission from their fellow worker and consumer councils to use particular productive resources which belong to all of us. All jobs include at least some tasks that are empowering and a mix of more and less pleasant tasks. Many needs are satisfied free of charge, however workers in each council decide if members deserve more or less compensation based on differences in efforts and sacrifices, and neighborhood consumption councils award extra consumption rights to members with special needs. Allocation of resources, labor, and intermediate goods to worker councils, as well as distribution of final goods and services to consumers is determined by a participatory planning procedure in which councils and federations of workers and consumers propose and revise their own activities under rules designed to guarantee outcomes that are efficient, equitable, and environmentally sustainable. There are no "classes" of people who share differently in the burdens and benefits of economic activity. Only to the degree that anyone shoulders greater burdens are they rewarded with greater benefits. Sound different?

Goals First

It is important when thinking about a desirable economy to start in the right place. First we should define our goals. We have to decide what kinds of human beings we want to become, what principles we want our economy to be based on, and only after that can we figure out what economic institutions and decision making procedures can best achieve our goals. The goals of a participatory economy are to achieve: *economic democracy*, defined as decision making power in proportion to the degree one is affected by a decision; *economic justice,* defined as economic reward commensurate with effort, sacrifice, and need; and *solidarity*, defined as concern for the wellbeing of others—all to be achieved without sacrificing economic *efficiency* while promoting a *variety* of economic life styles. Moreover, we understand that intergenerational equity and efficiency together imply that a participatory economy must be environmentally *sustainable*.

These goals guide us in designing rules and procedures for economic decision making. We want to build economic institutions and procedures that empower us to manage our own affairs, yield fair outcomes, promote concern for the wellbeing of others, protect the environment, and provide a diverse range of options for what to produce and consume, where and how to work, and who and how to be. And we want to do all this without wasting peoples' time and energy, or using scarce productive resources other than where they are most productive and valuable.

But we need to be more specific about how we define key goals. Sometimes disagreements about what institutions and procedures seem suitable stem from different ways of defining what economic justice, economic democracy, or sustainable means. Ambiguity about goals can prevent clear thinking about what is necessary to fulfill them and come back to bite us. The next four chapters explore our goals in greater depth.

CHAPTER FOUR

ECONOMIC DEMOCRACY

Who would dare come out and say they are against *economic democracy*? Who would say they are not in favor of people having control over their economic destinies? But what exactly does economic democracy mean?

Does it mean everyone should be free to do whatever they want with their person and property, including the right to enter into any contract they wish with anyone else? That is how conservatives like Milton Friedman define economic democracy, which they opportunistically call *economic freedom*.

The conservative concept of economic freedom is an inappropriate conception of economic democracy because many economic decisions affect more than one person. There are too many important situations where the economic freedom of one person conflicts with the economic freedom of another person. If polluters are free to pollute, victims of pollution are not free to live in pollution-free environments. If employers are free to use their productive property as they see fit, their employees are not free to use their laboring capacities as they like. If the wealthy are free to leave their children large bequests, new generations will not be free to enjoy equal economic opportunities. If those who own banks are free from a government-imposed minimum reserve requirement, ordinary depositors are not free to save safely. In sum, the goal of maximizing people's economic freedom over the "choice sets" that affect them is only meaningful in a context where people's choice sets do not intersect.

So it is not enough simply to shout "let economic freedom ring", as appealing as that may sound.

If the conservative concept of economic freedom is an inadequate and misleading conception of economic democracy in a world where one person's decision often affects others, what are the alternatives? The other dominant conception of economic democracy is *majority rule*. This concept was borrowed from political science where the notion that no citizen should have more say over political matters than any other was enshrined in the doctrine of one person one vote. The problem with majority rule is simple: When a decision has a greater affect on some people than others, by giving each person an equal vote, those more affected by a decision can find themselves overruled by those who are less affected. Even in the political sphere of social life, where there are many decisions that do affect all citizens more or less equally, there are some political decisions that clearly affect the lives of some citizens more than others, and some choices individuals should be allowed to make regardless of how much others may disagree and claim to be affected. In these circumstances political scientists sensibly amend the principle of majority rule with other concepts like a bill of rights, civil liberties, and supermajority voting rules.

But in the case of economic decisions the probability of unequal effects is much greater than in the case of political decisions. While there are some economic decisions that affect only a single person, and there are some economic decisions that affect us all roughly to the same extent, *most* economic decisions affect more than one person, but affect some people a great deal more than others. And therein lies the rub. While the concept of economic freedom works well for economic decisions that only affect one person, and the concept of majority rule works well for economic decisions that affect us all equally, neither conception of economic democracy works well for the overwhelming majority of economic decisions that affect some of us more than others.

This is why supporters of participatory economics think economic democracy should be defined as *decision making input, or power, in proportion to the degree one is affected by different economic choices.* We call this *economic self-management* and believe that thinking about achieving economic self-management for everyone is the best way to think about achieving economic democracy.

Obviously it will never be possible to arrange for decisions to be made so that every person enjoys perfect economic self-management. However, the goal of maximizing economic self-management as defined above is always meaningful, whereas the goal of maximizing people's economic freedom is not whenever an economic decision affects multiple parties (which it almost invariably does).

Of course agreeing on a definition and a goal is not the same as achieving the goal. Just because we have a clear definition of economic self-management, and just because this gives us a coherent goal to shoot for, does not mean we know how to achieve it. But getting clear about the goal is a first step in the right direction. As long as the phrase "economic democracy" remains vague, and is used to mean different things by different people, it is difficult to make progress toward achieving it. As long as people labor under a misconception about what economic democracy means, we will continue to search in the wrong directions. Thinking of economic democracy as individual economic freedom can lead us to embrace antidemocratic economic institutions like private enterprise and markets. While thinking of economic democracy as majority rule can blind us to the fact that even the most democratic version of central planning conceivable would still fail to let those who are more affected by a decision have more say over that choice.

CHAPTER FIVE

ECONOMIC JUSTICE

What is an equitable distribution of the burdens and benefits of economic activity? What reasons for compensating people differently are morally compelling, and what reasons carry no moral weight? While mainstream economists and the corporate media prefer to keep it off stage, the Occupy Movement has moved economic justice to center stage where it clearly belongs.

Four distributive principles, or "maxims," span the range of possible answers to the question of how people should be compensated for their part in economic cooperation:

- **Maxim 1**: *To each according to the value of the contribution of her human **and** physical capital.*

- **Maxim 2**: *To each according to the value of the contribution of **only** her human capital.*

- **Maxim 3**: *To each according to her effort, or personal sacrifice.* And,

- **Maxim 4**: *To each according to her need.*

Roughly speaking you can think of maxim 1 as the way conservatives would like us all to agree to define economic justice; maxim 2 as the way liberals tend to define economic justice; maxim 3 as how many economic justice activists define economic justice; and maxim 4 is the distributive principle that hopefully will blossom in a new world basking in the brilliant sunlight of resolute human solidarity.

Maxim 1: *To each according to the value of the contribution of her physical **and** human capital.* The rationale behind maxim 1 is that people should get out of an economy what they and their productive possessions contribute to the economy. If we think of economic goods and services as a giant pot of stew, the idea is that individuals contribute to how plentiful and rich the stew will be by their labor and by the non-human productive assets they bring to the economy kitchen. If my labor and productive assets make the stew bigger or richer than your labor and assets, then according to maxim 1 it is only fair that I eat more stew, or richer morsels, than you.

While this rationale has obvious appeal, it has a major problem we might call the *Rockefeller grandson problem*. According to maxim 1, the grandson of a Rockefeller with a large inheritance of productive property *should* eat a thousand times more stew than a highly trained, highly productive, hard working son of a pauper, even if Rockefeller's grandson doesn't work a day in his life and the pauper's son works for fifty years producing goods of great benefit to others. This will inevitably occur if we count the contribution of productive property people own, and if people own different amounts of machinery and land—or what is the same thing, different amounts of stocks in corporations that own the machinery and land—since bringing a stirring spoon, cooking pot, or stove to the economy kitchen increases the size and quality of the stew we can make just as surely as peeling the potatoes and stirring the pot does. So anyone who considers it *unfair* when the idle grandson of a Rockefeller consumes many times more than a hard working, productive son of a pauper cannot accept maxim 1 as her definition of economic justice.

But what if, unlike Rockefeller's grandson, those with more productive property acquired it through some merit of their own? Wouldn't contribution from productive property deserve reward in this case?

Besides inheritance, sometimes people acquire productive property through good luck. But unequal distributions of productive property that result from differences in luck are not the result of unequal sacrifices, unequal contributions, or any conceivable difference in merit between people. Good luck, by definition, is precisely *not* deserved, so any unequal incomes that result from unequal distributions of productive property due to differences in luck must be inequitable as well.

Another way people come to have more productive property is through unfair advantage. Those who are stronger, better connected, have insider information, or are more willing to prey on the misery of others can acquire more productive property through a variety of legal and illegal means. Obviously if unequal wealth is the result of someone taking unfair advantage of another, it is inequitable.

However, those who argue that owners of productive property deserve reward base their case on a different scenario. They consider the case where someone came to have more productive property than others by using income she earned fairly to purchase more productive property than others.

There is a difficult moral issue regarding income from productive property *even if* the property was purchased with income that we stipulate was fairly earned in the first place. Labor and credit markets allow people with productive wealth to capture part of the increase in productivity of *other people* that results when other people work with the productive wealth. To what extent the profit or interest owners of productive wealth receive initially is merited when they use their wealth to become employers or lenders should be carefully evaluated. But even if we stipulate that some compensation is justified by a meritorious action that occurred *once* in the past, it turns out that labor and credit markets allow those who own productive wealth to parlay it into *permanently* higher incomes which *increase* over time without further meritorious behavior on their parts. This creates the dilemma that ownership of productive property *even if justly acquired* may well give rise to additional income that becomes far greater than what is required to compensate its owner for her greater initial merit.[1]

In sum, for purposes of argument we can concede that *if* unequal accumulations of productive property were the result *only* of meritorious actions, *and if* compensation ceases when the meritorious action is fully compensated, rewards to property need not be unfair. But we should only consider such a concession if those who defend rewards to property concede in return that *if* those who own more productive property acquired it through inheritance, luck, unfair advantage, -- or because once they have more productive property than others they can accumulate even more by using labor or credit markets with no further meritorious behavior -- that unequal outcomes resulting from differences in wealth are unfair.

In any case, every empirical study of the origins of wealth inequality concludes that differences in ownership of productive property which accumulate within a single generation due to unequal sacrifices and/or unequal contributions people make themselves are quite small compared to the differences in wealth that develop due to inheritance, luck, unfair advantage, and accumulation. This means that the vast majority of returns to property cannot be considered fair. In this regard, as many sympathetic to the Occupy Wall Street Movement have come to realize, nothing has changed (unless for the worse) since the end of the nineteenth century when Edward Bellamy summarized the situation in his famous utopian novel, *Looking Backward,* as follows:

> *You may set it down as a rule that the rich, the possessors of great wealth, had no moral right to it as based upon desert, for either their fortunes belonged to the class of inherited wealth, or else, when accumulated in a lifetime, necessarily rep-*

---

1   For a simple model which highlights these dilemmas see Robin Hahnel, "Exploitation: A Modern Approach." *Review of Radical Political Economics 38, 2,* Spring 2006: 175-192.

resented chiefly the product of others, more or less forcibly or fraudulently obtained. – Edward Bellamy

Maxim 2: *To each according to the value of the contribution of **only** her human capital.* While those who support maxim 2 find most property income unjustifiable, advocates of maxim 2 hold that all have a right to what they call the "fruits of their own labor." The rationale for this has a powerful appeal: If my labor contributes more to the social endeavor it is only right that I receive more. Not only am I not exploiting others, they would be exploiting me by paying me less than the value of my personal contribution. But ironically, the same reason for rejecting maxim 1 applies to maxim 2 as well.

Economists define the value of the contribution of any input to production as the "marginal product" of that input. In other words, if we add one more unit of the input in question to all of the inputs currently used in a production process, how much would output increase? The answer is defined as the marginal product of the input in question. But mainstream economics teaches us that the marginal product, or contribution of an input, depends as much on the number of units of that input already in use, and on the quantity and quality of other, complimentary inputs, as on any intrinsic quality of the additional input itself. This fact undermines the moral imperative behind any "contribution based" maxim -- that is, maxim 2 as well as maxim 1.

But besides the fact that the marginal productivity of different kinds of labor depends largely on the number of people in each labor category in the first place, and on the quantity and quality of non-labor inputs available for use, most differences in people's personal productivities are due to intrinsic qualities of people themselves over which they have no control. No amount of eating and weight lifting will give an average individual a 6 foot 8 inch frame with 380 pounds of muscle. Yet professional football players in the United States receive hundreds of times more than an average salary because those attributes make their contribution outrageously high in the context of US sports culture.

The famous British economist, Joan Robinson, pointed out long ago that however "productive" a machine or piece of land may be, its productivity hardly constitutes a moral argument for paying anything to its owner. In a similar vein one could argue that however "productive" a 380-pound physique (or, for that matter, a high IQ) may be, that doesn't mean the owner of this trait deserves more income than someone less gifted who works just as hard and sacrifices as much. The bottom line is that the "genetic lottery" greatly influences how valuable a person's contribution will be. Yet the genetic lottery is no more fair than the inheritance lottery, and therefore maxim 2 suffers from the same flaw as maxim 1.

In defense of maxim 2 it is frequently argued that while talent may not deserve reward, talent requires training, and herein lies the sacrifice that merits reward. For example, it is often argued that doctors' high salaries are compensation for all their extra years of education. But longer training does not necessarily mean greater personal sacrifice. It is important not to confuse the cost of someone's training to society—which consists mostly of the *trainer's* time and energy, and scarce social resources like books, computers, libraries, and classrooms—with the personal sacrifice of the *trainee*. If teachers and educational facilities were paid for at public expense (that is, if we had a universal public education system) and if students were paid a living stipend (so they forego no income while in school) then the personal sacrifice of the student would consist only of her discomfort from time spent in school. But even in this case any personal suffering students endure must be properly compared. While many educational programs are less personally enjoyable than time spent in leisure, comparing discomfort during school with comfort during leisure is not the relevant comparison. In a universal public education system with living stipends, the relevant comparison would be between the discomfort students experience and the discomfort *others* experience who are working instead of going to school. If our criterion is greater personal sacrifice *than others*, then logic requires comparing the student's discomfort to whatever level of discomfort others are experiencing who work while the student is in school. Only if schooling is more disagreeable than working does it constitute a greater sacrifice than others make, and thereby deserve reward. So to the extent that the cost of education is borne at public rather than private expense, including the opportunity cost of foregone wages (as it will be in a participatory economy) and to the extent that the personal discomfort of schooling is no greater than the discomfort others incur while working, extra schooling merits no compensation on moral grounds.

In sum, we might call the problem with maxim 2 the *doctor-garbage collector problem.* How can it be fair to pay a brain surgeon who is on the first tee at his country club golf course by 1 PM even on the four days a week he works, ten times more than a garbage collector who works under miserable conditions forty plus hours a week if education is free and students are paid living stipends all the way through medical school? Despite the fact that many continue to search for reasons that returns to human capital are more justified than returns to physical capital, no reason holds up under careful scrutiny. Where does this difference in attitude many have toward rewards to physical and human capital come from?

No doubt the fact that the value of the contribution of our labor is the "joint product" of our human capital *and* our effort is responsible for part of the confusion. People *do* have some control over how valuable their labor contribution will be because we *do* have control over our effort. Whereas most people have little, if any control over how much physical capital we own, or how valuable its contribution will prove to be. Moreover, because our human capital only contributes when *we* work, and work often entails sacrifice, human capital cannot make any contribution unless its owner makes some sacrifices. On the other hand, when physical capital makes its contribution it is generally *not* its owner who makes any sacrifice, it is the owner's employees who work with the machinery and equipment and make the sacrifices associated with the contribution of the physical capital. But none of this is a reason to reward people according to the value of the contribution their human capital makes possible.

If we reward effort we reward the only thing people have control over, and if we reward people according to their sacrifices then we precisely compensate people for the sacrifices they make when their human capital makes a contribution. In other words, if we reward people according to their efforts and sacrifices, we have already taken care of the two reasons people rightly feel that reward according to the value of one's labor contribution is more just than reward for the value of the contribution of the physical capital one happens to own. However, once rewards have compensated people for differences in effort and sacrifice, to pay some more whose efforts were more productive *because* they were expended alongside greater amounts of human capital is no more fair than paying some more than others because the physical capital they own makes a more valuable contribution.

Maxim 3: Which brings us to maxim 3: *To each according to her effort, or personal sacrifice.* Whereas differences in contribution will be due to differences in talent, training, job assignment, luck, and effort, the only factor that deserves extra compensation according to maxim 3 is extra effort. By "effort" is meant personal sacrifice for the sake of the social endeavor. Of course effort can take many forms. It may be longer work hours, less pleasant work, or more intense, dangerous, unhealthy work. Or, it may consist of undergoing training that is less gratifying than the training experiences of others, or less pleasant than time others spend working who train less. The underlying rationale for maxim 3, which seems to be the view of most social justice activists, is that people should eat from the stew pot according to the sacrifices they made in cooking the stew. Compensation for above average sacrifices "evens things out" overall.

According to maxim 3 no other consideration, besides differential sacrifice, can justify one person eating more stew than another.

One argument for why sacrifice deserves reward is that people have control over how much they sacrifice. I can decide to work longer hours, or work harder, whereas I cannot decide to be 6 foot 8 or have a high IQ. It is commonly considered unjust to punish someone for something she could do nothing about. On those grounds paying someone less just because she is not large or smart violates a fundamental precept of fair play. On the other hand, if someone doesn't work as long or hard as the rest of us, we don't feel it is inappropriate to pay her less because she *could* have worked longer or harder if she had chosen to. In the case of reward according to effort, avoiding punishment is possible, whereas in the case of reward according to contribution it is largely unavoidable.

But are all people equally able to sacrifice? Or is it easier for some to make sacrifices than it is for others, just as it is easier for some to perform difficult and valuable physical or mental tasks than it is for others? Questions such as these make me happy I am not a philosopher! What can one say, except, "perhaps." But even if it is only a matter of degree, is it delusional to think it is usually easier for people to affect how much effort they put into a task, or how much they sacrifice for the common good, than it is for them to affect how valuable a contribution they make? We can leave philosophers to debate free will, but it is hard to believe we have no more control over our efforts and sacrifices than we do over how valuable our contribution will be.

In any case, there is no reason for society to frown on those who prefer to make fewer sacrifices as long as they are willing to accept less economic benefits to go along with their lesser sacrifice. Just because people enter into a system of equitable cooperation with others this does not preclude leaving the sacrifice/benefit trade-off to personal choice. Maxim 3 simply balances any differences in the burdens people choose to bear with commensurate differences in the benefits they receive.

This may be the strongest argument for reward according to sacrifice. Even if all were not equally able to make sacrifices, extra benefits to compensate for extra burdens seems fair. When people enter into economic cooperation with one another, for the arrangement to be fair should not all participants benefit equally? Since each participant bears burdens as well as enjoys benefits, it is equalization of *net* benefits, i.e. benefits enjoyed minus burdens born, that makes the economic cooperation fair. So if some bear more of the burdens justice requires that they be compensated with benefits commensurate with their greater sacrifice. Only then will all enjoy equal *net* benefits. Only then will the system of economic cooperation be treating all participants equally, i.e. giving equal weight or priority to the interests of all participants. Notice that even if some are more able to sacrifice than others, the outcome for both the more and less able to sacrifice is the same when extra sacrifices are rewarded. In this way all receive the same net benefits from economic cooperation irrespective of any differences in their abilities to contribute *or* to sacrifice.

Many who object to maxim 3 as a distributive principle raise questions about measuring sacrifice, or about conflicts between reward according to sacrifice and motivational efficiency. Since reward according to sacrifice and need is the distributive principle in a participatory economy we will have to consider these criticisms of maxim 3 very carefully in chapter 12. But notice that measurement problems, or conflicts between equity and motivational efficiency are *not* objections to maxim 3 as a conception of what is *fair*, i.e. they are *not* objections to maxim 3 *on equity grounds*. To reject maxim 3 because effort or sacrifice may be difficult to measure, or because rewarding sacrifice may conflict with "motivational efficiency" is not to reject maxim 3 because it is unfair. Later, when discussing incentives in chapters 12 and 15 it is argued that these reasons for rejecting maxim 3 are largely without merit. But no matter how weighty these arguments may or may not prove to be, they are not arguments against maxim 3 on grounds that it somehow fails to accurately express what it means for the distribution of burdens and benefits in a system of economic cooperation to be just, or fair. Even should it turn out that economic justice is difficult to achieve because it is difficult to measure something accurately, or costly to achieve because to do so generates inefficiency, one presumably would still wish to know exactly what this elusive and costly economic justice *is*.

In any economy there are always some who are unable to make contributions or sacrifices, and some who we believe should be exempted from doing so even if they are able. Disabilities prevent some people from being able to work, and we choose to exempt children and retirees from work as well. Whether we decide to base reward on contribution or sacrifice we must decide if some are exempt from whatever our general rule may be. Obviously there are issues of fairness to consider in any system of exemptions: (1) Are the rules for exempting people fair? (2) Are the rewards for those exempted fair? We will take up these rules for those exempted from work when discussing consumption rights in a participatory economy in chapters 12 and 13.

Of course proponents of maxims 1 and 2 reject maxim 3 because it fails to reward people according to the value of their contribution. Some whose contributions are of greater value may well receive no more than others whose contributions are less valuable in an economy where distribution is according to maxim 3. But we have found compelling reasons why contribution-based theories of economic justice fail to hold up under scrutiny: (1) Contribution-based notions of equity will necessarily punish some people for something they are powerless to do anything about. (2) Reward according to contribution—whether of one's productive property *and* person, or *only* of one's person—inevitably awards greater benefits to some who sacrificed less than others, and distributes less benefits to some who sacrificed more than others. In sum, there *is* a good answer to the question: "Why should those who sacrifice more benefit more?" The answer is: "Because otherwise people do not receive equal *net* benefits from the system of economic cooperation. Because otherwise the economic system does not give equal priority to everyone's interests. Because otherwise the economy does not treat people equally." But I know of no good answer to the question: "Why should those who contribute more benefit more?" The only answer to this question is the proverbial child's response – "Because."

Maxim 4: *To each according to her need.* Of course the more familiar phrasing of this maxim is "From each according to ability, to each according to need," and it was not only the maxim Karl Marx used to describe the distributive principle in a truly communist society, but also the maxim endorsed historically by many pre-Marxian socialists and by many anarchists ever since. The "official" distributive principle of a participatory economy is to reward people according to effort, or sacrifice, *and* need. Since this is different from distribution on the basis of need *only*, it is not surprising that it has become the subject of debate with some anarchists. This issue is treated at some length in chapters 12 and 15.

CHAPTER SIX

SUSTAINABILITY

It took a massive movement to raise the issue of whether or not economies were "environmentally sustainable," or instead, on course to destroy the natural environment upon which they depend. But it sometimes seems there are as many different definitions of "sustainability" and "sustainable development" as people who use the words. There are even some in the environmental movement who, with good reason, have suggested that "sustainable development" has become the enemy, rather than the friend, of the environment.

It is not clear that if we leave aside the question of how to popularize important ideas, there is anything in the notion of "sustainability" that is not already implicit in the goals of efficiency, equity, and variety. If an economy uses up natural resources too quickly, leaving too little or none for later, it is inefficient. If an economy sacrifices the basic needs of future generations to fulfill desires for luxuries of some in the present generation, it has failed to achieve intergenerational equity. If we chop down tropical forests with all their biodiversity and replace them with single species tree plantations, we have destroyed, rather than promoted variety.

Be this as it may, perhaps it is wise to adopt a principle the environmental movement has made famous: the *precautionary principle*. According to the precautionary principle, when there is fundamental uncertainty with very large downside risk, it is best to be cautious. In this case, it is by no means clear that the concepts of efficiency, equity, and variety include everything we need to consider regarding relations between the human economy and the natural environment. Since it is riskier to leave out the criterion of environmental sustainability than include it, it is best to include the goal of sustainability.

Weak sustainability requires only leaving future generations a stock of natural and produced capital that is as valuable, in sum total, as that we enjoy today. *Strong sustainability* requires, in addition, leaving future generations a stock of natural capital that is as valuable as that we enjoy. *Environmental sustainability* requires, in addition, leaving stocks of each important category of natural capital that are as large as those we enjoy. Obviously these are different notions of sustainability. The first allows for complete substitution between and within produced and natural capital. The second allows for substitution between different kinds of natural capital, as well as different kinds of produced capital, but not between natural and produced capital. The third does not permit substitution between different major categories of natural capital. After a lengthy chapter in another book[1] discussing a host of issues that make defining exactly what sustainability means difficult, I offered a formulation intended to get the major points across while making clear that the goal is by no means simple:

WHEREAS the natural environment provides valuable services both as the source of resources and as sinks to process wastes,

WHEREAS the regenerative capacity of different components of the natural environment and ecosystems contained therein are limited,

WHEREAS ecosystems are complex, contain self-reinforcing feedback dynamics that can accelerate their decline, and often have thresholds that are difficult to pinpoint,

WHEREAS passing important environmental thresholds

1   Robin Hahnel, *Green Economics: Confronting the Ecological Crisis* (M.E. Sharpe, 2011).

can be irreversible,

WE, the present generation, now understand that while striving to meet our economic needs fairly, democratically, and efficiently, we must not impair the ability of future generations to meet their needs and continue to progress.

IN PARTICULAR, WE, the present generation, understand that intergenerational equity requires leaving future generations conditions at least as favorable as those we enjoy. These conditions include what have been commonly called produced, human, and natural capital, ecosystem sink services, and technical knowledge.

SINCE the degree to which different kinds of capital and sink services can or cannot be substituted for one another is uncertain, and SINCE some changes are irreversible, WE, the present generation, also understand that intergenerational equity requires us to apply the precautionary principle with regard to what is an adequate substitution for some favorable part of overall conditions that we allow to deteriorate.

THEREFORE, the burden of proof must lie with those among us who argue that a natural resource or sink service that we permit to deteriorate on our watch, is fully and adequately substituted for by some other component of the inheritance we bequeath our heirs.

CHAPTER SEVEN
MORE GOALS

Efficiency

No word is as likely to turn off activists as "efficiency." As soon as efficiency is mentioned many activists tune out and head for the exits. This is understandable, but unfortunate. Understandable because many incorrectly use the word efficiency as if it were synonymous with profitability, which it is not. Understandable because mainstream economists often concentrate on efficiency and ignore other important criteria such as economic justice, economic democracy, solidarity, variety, and sustainability. Understandable because we are forever being told that whatever its other failings, free market capitalism is efficient—when our common sense tells us *correctly* that it is anything but!

However, rejecting efficiency as *one* goal, among others, is unfortunate, because as long as resources are scarce relative to human needs, and some socially useful labor is burdensome, efficiency is preferable to wastefulness. Radical activists should acknowledge that people have every reason to be resentful if their sacrifices are wasted, or if scarce social resources are squandered.

Economists prefer to define economic efficiency as *Pareto optimality*.[1] A Pareto optimal outcome is one where it is impossible to make anyone better off without making someone

---

1   Named after Vilfredo Pareto, 1848-1923.

else worse off. The idea is simply that it would be inefficient or wasteful not to implement a change that made someone better off and nobody worse off. Such a change is called a *Pareto improvement*, and another way to define a Pareto optimal, or efficient outcome, is as an outcome where no further Pareto improvements are possible. (Note: this standard definition of efficiency makes *no* mention of what is more or less profitable.)

This does not mean a Pareto optimal outcome is wonderful. If I have 10 units of happiness and you have 1, and if there is no way for me to have more than 10 unless you have less than 1, and no way for you to have more than 1 unless I have less than 10, then me having 10 units of happiness and you having 1 is a Pareto optimal outcome. But you would be right not to regard it very highly, and being a reasonable person, I would even agree with you. Moreover, there are usually *many* Pareto optimal outcomes. For instance, if I have 7 units of happiness and you have 6, and if there is no way for me to have more than 7 unless you have less than 6, and no way for you to have more than 6 unless I have less than 7, then me having 7 and you having 6 is also a Pareto optimal outcome. And we might both regard this second Pareto optimal outcome as better than the first. So the point is not that being in a Pareto optimal situation is necessarily wonderful; that depends on *which* Pareto optimal situation we're in. Instead the point is that *non*-Pareto optimal outcomes are undesirable because we could make someone better off without making anyone worse off, and it seems inefficient or wasteful not to do so. In short, it is hard to deny there is something wrong with an economy that systematically yields non-Pareto optimal outcomes, i.e., fails to make some of its participants better off when doing so would make nobody worse off.

It is important to recognize that the Pareto criterion, or definition of efficiency, is not going to settle most of the important economic issues we face. Most policy choices will make some people better off but others worse off, and in these situations the Pareto criterion has nothing to tell us. Consequently, if economists confined themselves to the narrow concept of efficiency as Pareto optimality, and only recommend policies that are, in fact, Pareto improvements, economists would have to be mute on most issues! For example, reducing greenhouse gas emissions makes a lot of sense because the future benefits of stopping global warming and avoiding dramatic climate change far outweigh the present costs of reducing emissions. But if even a few people in the present generation will be made somewhat worse off, even though many more people in future generations will be much, much better off, we cannot recommend the policy as a Pareto improvement—that is, on efficiency grounds in the narrow sense.

The usual way around this problem is to broaden the notion of efficiency from Pareto improvements to changes where the benefits to some outweigh the costs to others. This broader notion of efficiency is called the *efficiency criterion* and serves as the basis for cost benefit analysis. Simply put, the efficiency criterion says if the overall benefits to any and all people of doing something outweigh the overall costs to any and all people of doing it, it is "efficient" to do it. Whereas, if the overall costs to any and all people outweigh the overall benefits to any and all people of doing something, it is "inefficient" to do it. (Again, note: this definition of efficiency makes *no* mention of what is more or less profitable.)

Mainstream economists do not like to emphasize that policies recommended on the basis of the efficiency criterion are usually *not* Pareto improvements since they *do* make some people worse off. The efficiency criterion and all cost benefit analysis necessarily (1) "compares" different people's levels of satisfaction, and (2) attaches "weights" to how important different people's levels of satisfaction are when we calculate overall, *social* benefits and costs. Notice that when I stipulated that a few in the present generation might be worse off if we reduce greenhouse gas emissions while many will be benefited in the future, I was attributing greater weight to the gains of the many in the future than the loses of a few in the present. I think it is perfectly reasonable to do this, and do not hesitate to do so. But I am attaching weights to the well-being of different people, in this case roughly equal weights, which I also believe is reasonable. If one refuses to attach weights to the well-beings of different people, the efficiency criterion cannot be used. I also stipulated that the benefits of preventing global warming to people in the future were large compared to the cost of reducing emissions to people in the present. In other words, I was willing to compare how large a gain was for one person compared to how small a loss was for a different person. If one refuses to compare the size of benefits and costs to different people, the efficiency criterion cannot be used. In sum, unlike the narrow Pareto principle, the efficiency criterion requires comparing the magnitudes of costs and benefits to *different* people and deciding how much importance to attach to the well-being of *different* people.

In other words, applying the efficiency criterion requires *value judgments* beyond what are required by the Pareto criterion. So when mainstream economists pretend they have imposed no value judgments, and have separated efficiency from equity issues when they apply cost benefit analysis and recommend policy based on the *efficiency criterion,* they misrepresent themselves. While a Pareto improvement makes some better off at the expense of none—and therefore does not require comparing the sizes of gains and losses to different people or weighing the importance of well-being to different people—policies that satisfy the efficiency criterion generally make some better off precisely at the expense of others, which necessarily requires comparing the magnitudes of costs and benefits to winners and losers and making a value judgment regarding how important the interests of the winners are compared to the interests of the losers.

It is unfortunate that so many confuse economic efficiency with profitability even though they are not the same thing at all, and unfortunate when mainstream economist pretend they have made no value judgments when they engage in cost benefit analysis. But since it is undesirable when sacrifices we make when we work go wasted, or when limited social resources are misused, we do want our economy to be efficient as well as democratic, fair, and sustainable.

Solidarity

When proponents of participatory economics use the word **solidarity** we simply mean *concern for the well-being of others, and granting others the same consideration in their endeavors as we ask for ourselves.* Empathy and respect for others has been formulated as a "golden rule" and "categorical imperative," and solidarity is widely held to be a powerful creator of well-being. Solidarity among family members, between members of the same tribe, or within an ethnic group frequently generates well-being far in excess of what would be possible based on material resources alone. But in mainstream economics concern for others is defined as an "interpersonal externality" (a nasty sounding habit) and justification is demanded for why it is necessarily a good thing.

Sociability is an important part of human nature. Our desires develop in interaction with others. One of the strongest human drives is the never ending search for respect and esteem from others. All this is a consequence of our innate sociability. Because our lives are largely joint endeavors, it makes sense we would seek the approval of others for our part in group efforts. Since many of our needs are best filled by what others do for/ with us, it makes sense to want to be well regarded by others.

Now compare two different ways in which an individual can gain the esteem and respect of others. One way grants an individual status by elevating her above others, by positioning her in a status hierarchy that is nothing more than a pyramid of relative rankings according to established criteria, whatever they may be. For one individual to gain esteem in this way it is necessary that at least one other (and usually many others) lose esteem. We have at best a zero-sum game, and most often a negative sum-game since losers in hierarchies usually far outnumber winners.

The second way grants individuals respect and guarantees

that others are concerned for their well-being out of group solidarity. Solidarity establishes a predisposition to consider others' needs as if they were one's own, and to recognize the value of others' diverse contributions to the group's social endeavors. Solidarity is a positive-sum game. Any group characteristic that enhances the overall well-being members can obtain from a given set of scarce material resources is obviously advantageous. Solidarity is one such group characteristic. Clearly economic institutions that enhance feelings of solidarity are preferable to economic institutions that undermine solidarity among participants.[2]

Variety

Economic variety is defined as *achieving a diversity of economic life styles and outcomes*, and advocates of participatory economics believe it is desirable as an end as well as a means. The argument for variety as an economic goal is based on the breadth of human potentials, the multiplicity of human natural and species needs and powers, and the fact that people are neither omniscient nor immortal.

First of all, people are very different. The fact that we are all human means we have genetic traits in common, but this does not mean there are not differences among people's genetic endowments. So the best life for one is not necessarily the best life for another. Second, we are each individually too complex to achieve our greatest fulfillment through relatively few activities. Even if every individual were a genetic carbon copy of every other, the complexity of this single human entity, her multiplicity of potential needs and capacities, would require a great variety of different human activities to achieve maximum fulfillment. To generate this variety of activities

---

2   Only in societies as socially disoriented as ours is it necessary to "prove" something this obvious!

would in turn require a rich variety of social roles even in a society of genetic clones. And with a variety of social roles we would discover that even genetic clones would develop quite different derived human characteristics.

While these two arguments for the desirability of a variety of outcomes are "positive," there are "negative" reasons that make variety preferable to conformity. Since we are not omniscient nobody can know for sure which development path will be most suitable for her, nor can any group be certain what path is best for the group. John Stuart Mill astutely pointed out long ago in *On Liberty* that this implies that rather than repress heresy, the majority should be thankful to have minorities testing out different life styles, because every once in awhile every majority is wrong. Therefore, it is in the interest of the majority to have minorities testing their dissident notions of "the good life" in case one of them turns out to be a better idea. Finally, since we are not immortal, each of us can only live one life trajectory. Only if others are living differently can each of us vicariously enjoy more than one kind of life.

Now that we are clear about what our goals are – what we mean by economic democracy, economic justice, sustainability, efficiency, solidarity, and variety – we are ready to think about what kind of economic system can help us achieve them.

CHAPTER EIGHT

SOCIAL OWNERSHIP

In a participatory economy, society owns what has long been called "the means of production." Means of production include: Natural resources like arable land, forests, water, and minerals, as well as all the services various ecosystems provide; the buildings and facilities we call factories, together with all the machines and equipment inside them we use to manufacture different things; the skills different people have, like the ability to operate different pieces of equipment or to write computer code. In short, all of what economists like to call natural, produced, and human "capital."

The means of production also include the vast store of knowledge about how to go about producing different things with our means of production that every generation inherits as a "gift" from previous generations. All this cumulative knowledge, along with everything we require to set it in motion, belongs no more to one of us than it does to another. All of this belongs to all of us. We all have an equal right to decide how it is used. And we all have an equal right to benefit from whatever good derives from its use.

This doesn't mean you don't own your shoes, or that some guys in off-white jumpsuits are going to storm Grandma's apartment and confiscate her beloved fifty year-old radio. There will still be what is referred to as "personal property," which people "own" just as they do today. It simply means that what we need to produce all the goods and services we enjoy belongs to all of us. All these "means of production" and the knowledge of how to use them are treated as a gift from all who went before us to all of us alive today. It means we don't have a system where the vast majority who does not own their necessary means of production have no choice but to go to work for the tiny minority who owns what we need to work at a level of productivity our ancestors made possible. It means we don't have a handful of people who, because they own what the rest of us need to work, have a disproportionate say over what and how we will produce. It also means no one gets to extract a tribute from others before allowing them access to what they need to work productively. No profits. No rents. Instead everyone gets income based on the sacrifices they make in work as well as any special needs they may have, as will be explained.

This can be a difficult notion to grasp for people who have always lived in an economy where everything has an owner, because there really are no owners of our means of production in a participatory economy. Everybody and nobody owns the means of production. Instead, as explained later in chapter 14 on participatory planning, worker and consumer councils and federations grant "user rights" over particular parts of the means of production to one another through their participatory planning process in a way that ensures that all benefit equally from its deployment.

Yes, we certainly did have some bad experience with collective ownership of the means of production in twentieth century Communist economies. However, what collective ownership meant in those economies was that the state owned everything on behalf of the people, who then worked for the state under the direction of a small group of central planners and plant managers. That's not the kind of economy we are talking about at all—as will become apparent.

CHAPTER NINE

INSTITUTIONS

Councils—groups of people discussing and deciding together—have emerged in every major social revolution to date. In many cases those councils were soon destroyed. A good example is the Russian revolution where governance through *soviets* (Russian councils) and factory committees (where every worker had a vote) was replaced within a few years with rule by Bolshevik commissars. The most recent example is the Occupy Wall Street movement that quickly spread to over a thousand cities in the United States. In every occupation in every city a General Assembly, or GA, in which every participant has both voice and vote was the ultimate decision making body for the occupation. Whereas the major institutions that comprise a capitalist economy are limited liability corporations and markets, in a participatory economy the main institutions are two types of councils—worker councils and consumer councils—who together with federations of consumer and worker councils coordinate their interrelated activities through an institution we call participatory planning.

Worker Councils

All who are not too young, too old, or too disabled work somewhere. We ought to be able to participate in the process of deciding how our work will be organized. We ought to be able to decide together how much to work, under what conditions, at what times, to what end, and how to divide up various tasks among us. In order to have a say in how our workplace runs we should all be members of a council in our workplace. In a participatory economy a worker council is the ultimate decision making body in any workplace. Just as stockholder meetings, where each stockholder votes as many times as the number of shares of stock she owns, is "sovereign" in a capitalist corporation, the worker council, where each worker-member has one vote, is "sovereign" in a participatory economy.

Consumer Councils

We are also all consumers, and not just consumers of personal items like shirts, video games, and vacations at the beach. We are also consumers of neighborhood public goods like sidewalks and playground equipment at our neighborhood park, city wide public goods like libraries, mass transit, hospitals and schools, and state, regional, and national public goods like port facilities, bridges, national and state parks and forests, and yes, even national defense. In a participatory economy everyone is a member of her neighborhood consumer council where she (1) submits her personal consumption request, (2) participates directly in discussions about what neighborhood public goods to ask for, and (3) votes for recallable representatives to higher level federations of consumer councils at the ward, city, state, regional, and national levels, where delegates representing her discuss what higher level public goods to ask for.

One of the liabilities of market economies is that while they reduce what economists call the "transaction costs" people have to bear for individual consumption, they do nothing to lower the transaction costs of expressing one's preferences with regard to collective consumption. This generates a bias against collective consumption in favor of private consumption, which both reduces well-being and is environmentally destructive. By organizing consumers into councils and federations which participate on an equal footing with worker councils and federations in the participatory planning process, people are empowered as consumers not just as workers, and any bias against collective consumption is eliminated.

Federations of Councils

Federations of consumer councils are necessary because we need to decide what ward, city, state, regional, and national level public goods we want to consume. For somewhat different reasons explained later, federations of worker councils are also useful. While everyone can participate personally in the worker and neighborhood consumer council they belong to, unfortunately it is impractical for everyone to participate directly in deliberations in federations. Instead, councils must send representatives to deliberate in federations. For example, every neighborhood will send representatives to the city federation of neighborhood consumer councils, and it is these representatives who will discuss the relative merits of different city-wide public goods. Of course representatives can be rotated, subject to recall, or directed by their councils to vote a certain way if the councils they represent wish to do so. Moreover, federation decisions need not always be voted on by delegates, but can instead be decided by referenda where all members belonging to all councils that comprise the federation have a vote. In sum, while deliberation in worker and neighborhood consumer councils can and should be conducted through direct democracy, the deliberative work (although not necessarily the final decisions of federations) must be done through representative democracy.

Participatory Planning

In chapter 14 we explain how participatory planning works in detail. But it is important to note here that since individual worker and consumer councils participate directly in the planning procedure, all workers and all consumers also participate directly in formulating and revising their own council's proposals for what their council will do. In other words, the procedure for coordinating the interrelated activities of all the councils is one where councils participate directly, not by sending representatives to a planning body charged with coming up with a comprehensive plan on their behalf. As will become apparent, this distinguishes the participatory planning procedure not only from the central planning procedures used in Soviet type economies in the twentieth century, but also from all other proposals for how to carry out "democratic planning."

CHAPTER TEN

WORK: LIFE'S PRIME WANT?

Those who write about life after capitalism often dwell on how work can become desirable: a way in which people express their creativity, a means by which we fully develop our powers and potentials and express our solidarity with our fellow humans concretely by making things we know they will like. More than a hundred years ago Karl Marx speculated about a time when "labor has become not only a means of life but life's prime want," a time when "the subordination of the individual to the division of labor, and therewith also the antithesis between mental and physical labor, has vanished."[1]

Proponents believe work will both be, and feel different in a participatory economy because it will be organized and carried out very differently, as described in this and the next chapter. We also trust that once incentives are changed to prioritize finding new technologies that make work more pleasant and interesting for everyone it will quickly become more so. However, we also believe that tasks which are not pleasant, or intrinsically rewarding, will remain to be done. Sometimes it is inconvenient to have to show up to work on time, or remain longer than one would like, because those we work with need to be able to rely on us. In short, without prejudging how quickly, or to what extent work will become "life's prime want" (to be done simply because people find it more rewarding than whatever they would otherwise do in their leisure) we believe

---

1   Karl Marx, *Critique of the Gotha Program*, 1875.

that some aspects of work will require people to make what we call personal sacrifices for quite some time. In other words, we do not expect the issues of how sacrifices are to be distributed, what will motivate people to make sacrifices, and how those who make sacrifices in work are to be compensated to disappear for some time.

Worker Councils

In a participatory economy production is carried out by worker councils where each member has one vote. In a participatory economy all who work, and only those who work in the enterprise, have voice and vote in its governing body, the worker council, where all members have full and equal rights. In large enterprises worker councils will presumably find it helpful to establish smaller councils giving workers in different sub units a great deal of decision-making autonomy over decisions that mostly concern them. But whether or not to do this, and how to go about it, is ultimately up to the worker council where each worker has one vote.

Others have suggested giving "stake holders" seats on enterprise councils because people who do not work at an enterprise are often affected by enterprise decisions. And since winning "stake holders" a seat at the table is a reform we often must fight for in private enterprise market economies, many assume it is how the issue of enterprise effects on the broader "community" should be addressed in a desirable, post-capitalist economy as well. But there are two disadvantages to addressing the problem of community effects in this way: (1) How does one decide which other constituencies are affected, and how many seats to give them? It seems naïve to assume there would be no differences of opinion on these matters, and in absence of any objective criteria, decisions would be arbitrary even if not contentious. (2) If outsiders have seats, workers in an enterprise have no place where they can discuss what they want to do free from outside interference. Giving stake holders seats on the enterprise council requires workers to hear from, and convince outsiders before they can even formulate a proposal about what they want to do.

If the only way to enfranchise outsiders who are affected were to give them seats on enterprise councils, it might be necessary to achieve self-management as we have defined it. But the participatory planning procedure provides others who are affected an appropriate degree of influence over enterprise decisions without infringing on the autonomy of workers in the enterprise. As will be seen, the planning procedure empowers others to reject any proposal a group of workers makes that fails to benefit those outside the worker council at least as much as it costs them, and does so without arbitrarily deciding which outsiders are affected and to what degree. Limiting membership in worker councils only to workers in an enterprise does not mean they get to do whatever they want irrespective of its effects on others. As will become apparent, if a worker council votes to use productive resources belonging to everyone inefficiently, their proposal will not be approved in the participatory planning procedure. In other words, proponents of participatory economics believe the legitimate interests of others outside a workplace can be better protected through the participatory planning procedure than by giving outsiders seats on enterprise councils, which denies workers the right to function in a council where only they have voice and vote.

There is an ample literature documenting the advantages of employee self-management. Evidence is overwhelming that people with a say and stake in how they work not only find work more enjoyable, they are also more productive. So rather than dwell on the advantages of self-management (which should be beyond question) in the next two chapters we focus on two proposals about reorganizing work that have been the subject of much discussion among those who favor moving beyond capitalism.

CHAPTER ELEVEN

BALANCED JOBS

Every economy organizes work into jobs that define what tasks a single individual will perform. In hierarchical economies most jobs contain a number of similar, relatively undesirable, and relatively unempowering tasks, while a few jobs contain a number of relatively desirable and empowering tasks. But why should some people's work lives be less desirable than others? Doesn't taking equity seriously require balancing work for desirability? Proponents of participatory economics believe it does.

And why should work empower a few while disempowering most? If we want everyone to have an equal opportunity to participate in economic decision making, and if we want to ensure that a *formal* right to participate equally in worker councils translates into an *effective* right to participate equally, doesn't this require balancing work for empowerment? If some people sweep floors all week, year in and year out, while others evaluate new technological options and attend planning meetings all week, year in and year out, is it realistic to believe they have an equal opportunity to affect workplace decisions simply because they each have one vote in the worker council? Doesn't taking participation seriously require balancing work for empowerment? Again, proponents of participatory economics believe it does.

So in a participatory economy every worker councils is called upon to create a job balancing committee to distribute and combine tasks in ways that make jobs more "balanced" with regard to desirability and empowerment. The reaction against balanced job complexes from not only mainstream but many progressive economists as well has been fierce.

> *Apart from their inhibition of personal freedom, balanced job complexes designed to avoid specialization seem likely to deprive society of the benefits of activities performed well only by people who have devoted a disproportionate amount of time and effort to them. --Thomas Weisskopf*

> *Personal endowments as well as preferences differ greatly. Up to a point, specialization provides important efficiency gains. A certain level of specialization and hierarchy seems necessary and functional to me. -- Nancy Folbre*

Balanced jobs are designed to avoid disparate empowerment and thereby protect the freedom of those who otherwise would not have equal opportunity to participate in economic decision making. Balanced jobs are designed to prevent class divisions. But balanced jobs do *not* eliminate specialization. The proposal is not that everyone perform every task, which is impossible and ridiculous. Each person will still perform a very small number of tasks in her particular balanced job. Some will still specialize in brain surgery, others in electrical engineering, others in high voltage welding, etc. But if the specialized tasks in a job are more empowering than tasks are on average, those who perform them will also perform some less empowering tasks as well. And if the specialized tasks in a job are more desirable than tasks are on average, those who perform them will also perform some less desirable tasks -- unless they wish to work more hours or consume less because they have made fewer sacrifices.

The tasks each person performs only need to be balanced for empowerment and desirability over a reasonable period of time. Jobs do not have to be balanced every hour, or every day, or every week, or even every month. The balancing is also done in the context of what is practical in particular work situations. Technologies and worker capabilities and preferences must all be taken into account when balancing jobs in any worker council. Finally, the balancing is done by committees composed of workers in each work place, and done as they see fit. Jobs are not balanced by an external bureaucracy and imposed on workers. So proponents believe there is every reason to expect that job balancing committees composed of workers in a workplace will take ample leeway in organizing work to accommodate technological, skill, and psychological considerations while eliminating the kind of large, persistent differences in empowerment and desirability that characterize work life today. Nonetheless, critics have repeatedly raised two objections that deserve consideration:

Talent is scarce and training is socially costly, therefore it is inefficient for talented people, or people with a great deal of training, to do "menial" tasks.

The "scarce talent" argument against balancing jobs makes a valid point. However, the objection is usually greatly overstated. It is true not everyone has the talent to become a brain surgeon, and it is true there are social costs to training brain surgeons. Therefore, there *is* an efficiency loss whenever a skilled brain surgeon does something other than perform brain surgery. Roughly speaking, if brain surgeons spend X% of their time doing something other than brain surgery, there is an additional social cost of training X% more brain surgeons.

But as noted, virtually every study confirms that participation not only increases worker satisfaction, it increases worker productivity as well. So if balanced jobs enhance effective participation (as they are intended to) the efficiency loss because they fail to economize on "scarce talent" completely, must be weighed against the productivity gain they bring from greater participation of all workers. Then, if there is still a net efficiency loss, this would have to be weighed against the importance of balancing jobs for empowerment in giving people equal opportunities to exercise self-management in work.

For everyone to participate equally in economic decisions ignores the importance of expertise.

The "expertise" argument against balancing jobs for empowerment fails to distinguish between the legitimate role of expertise and an unwarranted usurpation of decision making power by experts. In circumstances where the consequences of decisions are complicated and not readily apparent, there is an obvious need for experts. But economic choice entails both determining *and* evaluating consequences. Presumably those with expertise in a matter can predict the consequences of a decision more accurately than non-experts. But those affected by a choice know best whether they prefer one outcome to another. So, while efficiency requires an important role for experts in predicting consequences of choices in complicated situations, efficiency also requires that those who will be affected determine which consequences they prefer. This means not only is it inefficient to prevent experts from explaining consequences of complicated choices to those who will be affected, it is also inefficient to keep those affected by decisions from making them after considering expert opinion. Self-management, defined as decision making input in proportion to the degree one is affected by the outcome, does not mean there is no role for experts. Instead it means confining experts to their proper role and keeping them from usurping a role that it is neither fair, democratic, nor efficient for them to assume.

In sum, proponents of participatory economics believe there is ample leeway in organizing work to accommodate practical considerations while eliminating *persistent* differences in empowerment and uncompensated differences in desirability.

CHAPTER TWELVE

REWARDS FOR EFFORT

As already explained, it will be necessary for people to make sacrifices in work for some time. This is why it is recommended that worker councils provide each member with what is called an "effort rating." The purpose is to recognize that not everyone always makes equal sacrifices in work, and those who make greater sacrifices are entitled to compensation in the form of extra consumption rights.

Worker councils need not go about rating members in the same way, any more than they have to organize their work and balance their jobs in the same way. In fact, in a participatory economy there is only one restriction placed on how a worker council can assign members effort ratings. In order to avoid the temptation for workers to award each other higher ratings than they truly believe each other deserve in exchange for like treatment by their workmates, the average effort rating councils award their members needs to be capped. One could give the same caps to all worker councils. Or, alternatively, one could set each council's average effort rating equal to 100 times the ratio of the social benefits of its outputs to the social costs of its inputs, as will be explained later in chapter 14 where the participatory planning procedure is explained. These rules for capping average effort ratings have different advantages and disadvantages as discussed in chapter 15, but as long as the average effort ratings of councils are capped we need not fear "effort rating inflation."

As in the case of balancing jobs for desirability and empowerment, many have expressed concerns about rewarding effort, and problems that may arise when efforts are judged by one's work mates.

First, it is very difficult to observe and measure an individual's sacrifice or work effort. Moreover, people would have an interest in understating their natural talents and abilities. Second, while it would elicit greater work effort and sacrifice, it would do nothing to assure that such effort and sacrifice were expended in a desirable way. -- Thomas Weisskopf

A society seeking optimum production needs to discourage clumsy effort and encourage proficient effort so as to avoid waste. Otherwise, the less successful have no material incentive to modify bungling methods. -- Mark Hagar

Maximizers would have incentives to perform at less than their best in early stages in order to maximize later effort score.... A standard strategic move to maximize winnings over a series of handicap races is to intentionally perform badly in early races in order to get a better handicap in later ones. -- John O'Neill

Anyone who has participated in a workplace with more than two or three workers knows the problem of cliques and rivalries that tends to arise. It is not clear how one would prevent cliques and rivalries from intruding into the effort evaluation process. -- David Kotz

Before addressing these concerns, let me dispose of a common misconception about participatory economics and what are often called "material rewards." Many critics have jumped to the conclusion that there are no material incentives for workers in a participatory economy. This is simply not true. People do not receive equal consumption for *un*equal efforts in a participatory economy. People's efforts are rated by their co-workers, and people are awarded consumption rights according to those effort ratings. To each according to her effort means there are material rewards for above average efforts and material consequences for below average efforts.

However, differences in people's efforts will not lead to the extreme income differentials characteristic of all economies today, nor the degree of income inequality predictable in market socialist economies. Therefore material incentives will play a smaller role in participatory economies than they do in other economies. Moreover, supporters believe a participatory economy can *eventually* lead to more and more distribution on the basis of need, that is, to a gradual reduction of material incentives. What reasons are there to expect any of this to be the case?

In a society that awards esteem mostly on the basis of what the American economist Thorstein Veblen famously termed "conspicuous consumption," it is hardly surprising that large income differentials are considered necessary to induce effort. But to assume that only conspicuous consumption can motivate people because under capitalism we have strained to make this so is unwarranted. There is plenty of evidence that people can be moved to great sacrifices for reasons other than a desire for personal wealth. Family members make sacrifices for one another without the slightest thought of material gain. Patriots die to defend their country for little or no pay. And there is good reason to believe that for people who are not pathological, wealth is generally coveted only as a *means* of attaining other ends such as economic security, comfort, respect, status, or power. If accumulating disproportionate consumption opportunities is often a means of achieving more fundamental rewards, there is good reason to believe a powerful system of incentives need not be based on widely disparate consumption opportunities when basic needs are guaranteed and fundamental desires are rewarded directly rather than indirectly.

If expertise and excellence are accorded social recognition directly, as they are in a participatory economy, there should be less need to employ the intermediary of conspicuous consumption. If economic security is guaranteed, for everyone, as it is in a participatory economy, there should be no need to accumulate out of fear for the future. If the material, medical, and educational needs of one's children are provided for at public expense, as they are in a participatory economy, there should be no need to accumulate to guarantee one's children the opportunities they deserve. Moreover, if people design their own jobs and participate in economic decision making, as they do in a participatory economy, they should carry out their responsibilities with less need for external motivation of any kind. And if the distribution of burdens and benefits is fair, as it is in a participatory economy, people's sense of social duty should be a more powerful incentive than it is today.

In other words, while a participatory economy does have material incentives, it is designed to maximize the motivating potential of many non-material incentives as well. Supporters think there is good reason to believe these non-material incentives can play a much bigger role in a participatory economy than they do today. But there is no way to "prove" that material rewards may be less necessary to motivate effort in different social circumstances than we are accustomed to. Nor do I expect to convince skeptics in a few paragraphs. But it is important to pose the question skeptics raise accurately: If medical, retirement, and children's expenses are taken care of at social expense, if valuable contributions are awarded public recognition, if people plan and agree to their tasks themselves, if a fair share of effort and personal sacrifice are demanded by workmates who must otherwise pick up the slack, *and* if extra effort is rewarded by commensurate increases in consumption opportunities, will people still be insufficiently motivated to do what needs to be done without larger income differentials than are permitted in a participatory economy? In any case, *that* is the relevant question. Now to address critics' specific concerns.

Weisskopf gives voice to the common assumption that effort is difficult, if not impossible to measure, while the value of a worker's contribution can be measured easily. But neither half of this proposition is as compelling as usually presumed. Assigning responsibility for outcome in group endeavors is often ambiguous. Sports teams are more suited to such calibration than production teams. And compared to football, soccer, and basketball, it is easiest to calibrate the value of individual contribution to group achievement in baseball. But even in baseball, debates over different measures of offensive contribution, like batting average, on base percentage, runs batted in, slugging percentage, etc., as well as disagreements over the relative importance of pitching versus hitting versus fielding, not to speak of arguments over what are called "intangibles" and "team chemistry," testify to the difficulty of assigning individual responsibility for group success. Moreover, it is usually more difficult, not less, to assign individual responsibility to different workers than to different athletes for the accomplishments of their "teams."

Nor is measuring effort as impossible as Weisskopf and others presume. Anyone who has taught and graded students for long knows there are two different ways to proceed. Teachers can compare students' performances on tests and papers to some abstract standard in the teacher's head, or, more realistically, to each other's performances. Alternatively, teachers can compare a student's performance to how well we expect the student to be able to do on an assignment. We can ask: Given the student's level of preparation when she entered the class, given the student's natural ability, is this an A, B, or C effort on the assignment *for this student*? This kind of question is not one teachers find impossible to answer.

Moreover, it should be easier for workmates to judge each others' efforts than it is for teachers to judge students' efforts. By and large teachers do not observe their students' efforts. On the other hand, in a participatory economy a worker's effort is judged by people who do the same kind of work, people who often work next to and in collaboration with her, and people who are familiar with how she has worked in the past. For all these reasons it should be easier for workmates to judge one another's efforts than it is for teachers to judge students' efforts.

While we believe worker councils would take the task of effort rating seriously since it affects how much consumption each is entitled to, we do not expect all worker councils to approach the task of effort rating in the same way. Some groups of workers may decide they only want to make rough distinctions between people's effort – and simply rate below average, average, and above average. While other groups might want to draw much finer distinctions -- perhaps giving everyone a score between zero and two hundred, with one hundred the average score. No doubt worker councils will use different procedures to judge one another's efforts. The number of people on the effort rating committee, their term of office, rules for rotation, the grievance procedure, and the amount of time spent observing others, versus collecting testimony from workmates, versus self-testimony will no doubt vary from worker council to worker council.

Presumably one thing people will consider when deciding where they want to apply to work in a participatory economy will be whether they feel comfortable with the way a worker council they join goes about rating effort. Do I like the degree of gradation? Do I trust the system? Do I think they spend too much or too little time judging one another's efforts? Proponents of participatory economics expect these are questions job applicants will ask about alternative places to work, just as we expect dissatisfaction with the effort rating process will be among the reasons people leave employment in one worker council and seek it in another. Ultimately the question is not whether people's efforts, or personal sacrifices in work, will be perfectly estimated because, of course, they will not be. Instead the question is if most people will feel they are being treated fairly most of the time, and if not, if people feel they have reasonable opportunities for redress.

Weisskopf, Hagar and O'Neill all ask if there are sufficient incentives in a participatory economy to ensure that people will exert themselves in socially useful ways. But why would one's co-workers reward clumsy, bungling, or misdirected effort rather than proficient effort? Why would fellow workers have any less incentive to discourage ineffective, and encourage effective effort on the part of co-workers than capitalist employers do? Every effort rating committee is constrained by a fixed average effort rating for all workers in their council. Therefore, rewarding inefficient effort on the part of a co-worker is just as detrimental to the interests of other workers in the council as it would be if they deliberately overstated a worker's effort. While those serving on effort rating committees will surely consider co-workers' contributions as *one piece of evidence* in estimating how hard a workmate is trying to be effective, the difference is that in a participatory economy they will take other factors into account as well, because simply rewarding the value of someone's contribution is not fair. Who are better than her co-workers to know if a worker is charging off at breakneck speed without checking to see if her exertions are effectively directed? Who is in a better position to judge if someone habitually engages in "clumsy effort?" Who can better tell if someone only gives the appearance of trying? Not only are co-workers in the best position to make these judgments, fellow workers in a worker council in a participatory economy have just as much incentive to discourage these kinds of behaviors as do capitalist employers or managers of market socialist enterprises.

Weisskopf and O'Neill also worry that people will try to disguise their true abilities to trick workmates into giving them higher effort ratings than they deserve. It is true that competitors in a series of races which they know will be handicapped may have an incentive to go slow in early races to inflate their handicap advantages in later ones. But again, remember who is judging effort in a participatory economy. Who is in a better position to know if someone is deliberately under performing in the beginning than the people working with her in the same kind of task? We should also ask how much damage is done if someone does pull the wool over her work mates' eyes through this stratagem. There is an efficiency loss from deliberate under performance in early races as well as an injustice because later efforts are overestimated and over rewarded. But rewarding place of finish is even more unfair because it penalizes the less able for something they cannot do anything about. Rewarding place of finish is also less efficient since it provides no incentive to improve performance if an improvement is insufficient to pass a rival. Is it really a fatal flaw if some devious-minded worker in a participatory economy tries to underperform early in order to be overpaid later?

Finally, Kotz worries that cliques and rivalries will lead to inequities and mistrust in participatory workplaces. Why might this be true? Cliques attempt to bias judgments that are the basis for reward. If reward were according to weight, and if all workers were weighed on the same scale, in public view, there would be no reason for cliques to arise because it would be impossible to contest judgments. Or, if reward were according to personal whim, but there was no way to discover the identity of the judge whose whim a clique would have to influence, there would also be no basis for cliques. So the problem with reward according to effort as judged by one's co-workers is that people's efforts *are* subject to question, and everyone knows whose opinion matters. Moreover, if all rotate on to and off of the effort rating committee, those serving now know those they judge will judge them later. "Payback" and "tit-for-tat" are phrases that spring to mind. Can the problem of cliques be avoided?

I don't think it is possible to eliminate differences of opinion about effort or sacrifice. And, unfortunately, economic justice requires compensating for differences in effort or sacrifice, not differences in weight! So unless we are prepared to foreswear attempts to reward people fairly, the best that can be done in this regard is to explore ways to diminish problems that arise due to differences of opinion. Many assume the only way to reduce disagreement about workers' relative efforts is to improve the accuracy of measurement. This is one strategy: (1) Collect more and better evidence, and weigh it more judiciously. However there are two additional strategies that can be pursued as well: (2) Improve "due process" so people are less resentful even when they disagree with judgments. Disagreements are problematic to the degree that they breed resentment. (3) Reduce the importance of the entire issue relative to other issues. Even if there are disagreements over judgments, and even if there is dissatisfaction over process, if the question of effort rating is farther down people's list of priorities, the consequences will be less problematic. I recognize that these are palliatives rather than cures. I began by admitting that perfect measurement is impossible. Moreover, I realize that my second suggestion amounts to searching for ways to make people more accepting of what they believe to be unfair, and my third suggestion amounts to trying to make people worry less about about economic injustice in general.

However, there is an important difference between economies that systematically practice injustice and an economy that is organized to distribute the burdens and benefits of economic activity as fairly as is possible. And there is good reason to believe people's attitudes about distributive justice would be somewhat different in those different contexts. If people believe the economic system is fair, might they not be inclined to attach less importance to disagreements over distributive outcomes in general? If workers believe their own council practices due process, might they not be more tolerant when they disagree with their effort rating committee? More concretely, is there no reason to believe people might be less inclined to form cliques and engage in rivalry when the overall system is fair, and when workers in every council have it within their power to modify procedures until they are satisfied there is "due process" if not perfect justice? In general, is it unreasonable to hope that the more economic justice people experience, and the longer justice prevails over injustice, the less people will choose to spend their time and energy in invidious comparisons, at least regarding the distribution of consumption rights over material possessions?

It is possible to immunize judges from pressures coming from those they judge, but I fear the disadvantages of doing so in this context would far outweigh the advantages, and therefore do not recommend it. Outsiders could be brought in to judge efforts, workers from other worker councils in the same industry federation being obvious candidates. But outside judges reduce self-management for workers in their councils. In other words, the main problem with outside judges is precisely that they are outsiders. Do we want self-management or not? Alternatively, the identity of co-workers serving on the effort ratings committees could be kept secret to protect them from influence. While secrecy may appear attractive, I am deeply skeptical that this would minimize rather than maximize the problem of cliques. Besides a host of theoretical reasons that open and easy access to information for all is good policy, and besides the fact that good legal systems recognize the importance of those charged being able to know their accusers, there is a major practical reason that secrecy is bad policy. Namely, it doesn't work! More often than not it turns out that what one blithely assumed could be kept secret, actually was not kept secret. So what we usually must choose between is openness versus pretense of secrecy, whether we realize it or not. In this case, the advantages of openness over pseudo-secrecy *visa vis* cliques and rivalries seem obvious.

In sum, critics raise important issues I would not belittle. In the end I can only say: (1) Estimating the value of people's contributions to collaborative outcomes is also an imperfect science and subject to question. (2) While proponents of participatory economics *recommend* rewarding effort as an equitable social norm that is compatible with efficiency, in the end we *propose* that individual worker councils rate their members as they see fit, and expect they will go about it in very different ways. (3)

Finally, perhaps the best defense for having co-workers judge one another's efforts at work is the defense Winston Churchill offered for democratic government: "No one pretends that democracy is perfect.... Democracy is the worst form of government except for all the others." In a similar vein, while effort rating by co-workers will no doubt prove difficult and quarrelsome at times, failing to monitor and reward effort, or judging workers on some basis other than their efforts, or assigning someone other than one's workmates as judges would be much worse. In short, our critics no doubt are right: remuneration according to effort, or sacrifice, as judged by one's co-workers is the worst possible system of compensation...except for all the alternatives!

Mark Hagar raises a further question about incentives to train oneself worthy of consideration:

> *Society needs to encourage people to prepare themselves to work where their comparative advantage in contribution is greater. For efficiency, one must reward efforts to improve the success of efforts, and rewarding contribution may be the only feasible way to do so. – Mark Hagar*

Hagar is absolutely correct that efficiency requires that people educate and train themselves in ways they can be most socially useful. Taken to its logical extreme we could even say there is both an efficient *amount* of education and training each person should receive, and an efficient *distribution* of that training and education over particular programs of study. Of course when put this way the implications of efficiency for education and training might seem a little frightening since most of us like the idea that we should be able to *choose* to study what we like. Regarding education and training, how are personal choice and efficiency reconciled in a participatory economy?

All education and training is paid for at public expense, including appropriate living stipends for students. All are free to apply to any educational and training programs they wish. In a participatory economy applicants are admitted on the basis of merit using the best predictors available for success in a program, tempered, of course, by affirmative action quotas when necessary to correct for racial and gender biases due to historical discrimination. The key questions are how the number of positions in different educational programs are determined, and what the personal consequences of acceptance and rejection are.

Education is both a consumption and an investment good, so the number of positions in programs should be determined both by how much people enjoy different kinds of education, *and* by how much different kinds of education improve people's social productivity. But how should acceptance or rejection into educational programs affect people? When answering this question it is important to ask who is paying for people's education, and what those who do not spend more time in educational programs are doing instead. As explained, in a participatory economy education is at public rather than private expense. If those who spend less time in educational programs were enjoying more leisure time, and if studying were less desirable than leisure, then those who study longer would deserve extra compensation commensurate with their extra sacrifice. However, as is more often the case, if those who spend less time in educational programs are working while other members of their age cohort are going to school longer, then those who study longer deserve no extra compensation, except in the unlikely event that time spent studying is more undesirable than time spent working.

Since remuneration is based on effort and sacrifice rather than productivity in a participatory economy, the expected income of those who spend more time in education will not be higher than the expected income of those with less. In other words, acceptance or rejection into education and training programs -- beyond the years of education all receive -- should have no appreciable effect on people's income prospects in a participatory economy. However, this does not mean that acceptance or rejection does not affect people's lives.

If I am accepted into a program of study I like, presumably this improves the quality of my life. If I am accepted into an educational program that qualifies me for a job with tasks I prefer, this improves the quality of my work life. Finally, if I am accepted into an educational program that makes my contributions more valuable this will earn me greater social recognition and appreciation from my fellow workers and the consumers we serve. Since a participatory economy is not an "acquisitive" society where people are judged by their belongings, but a society in which esteem and respect are won through "social serviceability," there should be strong social incentives to develop one's most socially useful potentials through education and training. In sum, while there are no material incentives in the form of extra consumption privileges to be gained from pursuing more years of socially useful education and training, there are no material *dis*incentives, and there are significant personal benefits.

No doubt some will worry that even under these circumstances the absence of material rewards for accumulating "human capital" in a participatory economy will fail to lead people to sufficiently pursue their education and training, while others may complain that those who are rejected by educational programs in a participatory economy are unfairly penalized by non-material losses. I seriously doubt there would be a dearth of applicants to colleges, graduate programs, or medical schools in a participatory economy. When it is apparent the alternative to education is work, not leisure, study suddenly has a way of appearing less burdensome! While those who do not qualify for extra education and training may suffer unfairly because they cannot pursue a course of study they would enjoy, or work at a job with tasks they prefer, this injustice is much less than occurs in economies where remuneration is based on the value of one's contribution which depends on education, rather than on the sacrifices one makes. More-

over, proponents of participatory economics know of no way
to avoid this inequity, and it may be necessary to assure that
people do seek to educate themselves in socially useful ways as
Hagar reminds us.

What About Need?

How might an economy fail to distribute goods and services in a way that is beyond moral reproach? Proponents of
participatory economics believe that ignoring differences in
sacrifice would be immoral. We also believe that ignoring differences in need is morally unacceptable. But there are two
ways to think about and pose these objections. One is to describe either failure as "unjust." In effect this makes "economic
justice" and "morally acceptable" synonymous. The other way
is to draw a distinction between what it means for an economy
to be *just* and what it means for an economy to be *humane*. In
this usage it is conceivable that a just economy—which provides compensation commensurate with people's efforts and
sacrifices—might fail to be humane by denying those with
greater needs what they require. In this usage it is also possible that a humane economy— which compensates all with
greater needs appropriately—might fail to treat people fairly;
for example, by rewarding people on the basis of the contribution of their person and property rather than their efforts and
sacrifices.

The important thing is to agree that any economy that
fails on *either* score is morally unacceptable, in which case
the policy implications are the same no matter whether or
not one chooses to draw a distinction between "just" and "humane." Since proponents of participatory economics endorse
an economy that is both just and humane, i.e. an economy
beyond moral reproach of any kind, we support distributing
consumption rights according to effort (or sacrifice) *and* need,
which is the "official" distributive principle in a participatory

economy. This "official principle" is implemented by tasking worker councils with deciding if there are any differences in the efforts of their members they wish to report (as discussed in this chapter) and tasking neighborhood consumption councils with deciding if there are any differences in the needs of their members which should be taken into account (as explained next chapter).

Some anarchists have criticized participatory economics because they favor the distributive principle "to each according to need," even if "from each according to ability" cannot be assumed to apply in full. Fortunately, I do not believe this disagreement matters for two reasons.

It doesn't matter because in a participatory economy what is proposed is that each worker council decide for itself how to rate its members' efforts. As already explained, proponents of participatory economics are under no illusions that every group of workers will decide to go about this in exactly the same way. Not only will different worker councils decide on different procedures, (rules for who serves on the rating committees, what information the committee collects, grievances procedures, etc.) they may also decide to apply different criteria. So any group of workers who wished to accept members' self-declarations about their own efforts, or who wished to report no differences of effort among their members, is free to do so. Nobody will interfere or think any the worse of them for doing so.

It also doesn't matter because in a participatory economy what is proposed is that, beyond making some goods and services like education, medical care, and access to recreational facilities free of charge, each neighborhood consumption council decide for itself how to take any differences in the needs of its members into account when approving consumption requests. So if neighbors are willing to accept one another's self-declarations regarding special needs they are free to do so. And again, nobody will interfere or think the worse of them for doing so.

So there is no need to speculate about what people in general will feel like doing when the time comes. If people have sufficient trust in one another to allow others to self-declare what their needs are, and consume on that basis without regard to effort, then they will go ahead and do so. If, on the other hand, people want to protect themselves against the possibility of socially irresponsible behavior of others (as I suspect many will, at least in the beginning) then they will do so by linking consumption rights to effort and sacrifice in work in their worker councils, and reviewing requests for extra consumption due to greater need in consumption councils rather than accepting peoples' self-need assessments without question. However, let me be clear: The sooner people develop more solidarity, and are therefore willing to dispense with protective procedures, the better as far as I am concerned. Moreover, I have yet to meet an advocate of participatory economics who feels differently.

No Labor Markets!

In a participatory economy everyone is free to apply for work in any worker council of their choice, or form a new worker council with whomever they want. But how does this really work? How would it be different from labor markets today?

In some centrally planned economies during the twentieth century people were assigned to work in particular state enterprises and not free to move to another. In many "patriarchal" Japanese corporations people work their entire lives for the same corporation of necessity because other Japanese firms hire only from new entrants in the labor market. In the United States certain occupations were closed to African Americans and women before the Equal Economic Opportunity Act outlawed discrimination in employment. Moreover, empirical evidence strongly suggests that occupational segregation continues to remain more than forty years after the passage of this landmark civil rights legislation.

In other words, even when everyone is free to apply for work wherever they wish, this "freedom" can be an empty formality if the probability of success is very low. In third world economies, jobs in the formal sector have long been so few compared to the supply of labor being expelled from traditional agriculture that anyone fortunate enough to have a job in the formal sector would do anything to keep it to avoid a precarious existence in the informal sector. Now that ruling elites in Europe and North America have made it quite clear that they have abandoned full employment as a goal, many laid off in the Great Recession will not get their jobs back, and many more leaving the educational system will discover there are no jobs for them. So while freedom to apply for work wherever one wishes is important, if there are not enough good jobs to go around, there will always be some who are disappointed.

One advantage of planned economies compared to market economies is they can more easily provide full employment. The participatory planning procedure described in chapter 14 generates an annual plan that contains jobs for everyone in the labor force doing socially useful work they are trained and qualified for: No "cyclical unemployment" due to too little demand for goods and services to warrant hiring everyone. No "structural unemployment" because people's skills do not match job qualifications. These reasons that labor is often unemployed or underemployed in market economies are ironed out during the participatory planning process, rather than left to chance to be sorted out imperfectly in "real time."

But how do people get matched with jobs in a participatory economy? An approved production plan authorizes a worker council to employ a certain number of members with particular skills. Given who is already working there and the skills they have, this means the council may have to add members, layoff members, or exchange members for others with different skills. The personnel department lists any new openings they have, and chooses from among those who apply. New entrants to the labor force and laid off workers consult the list of new jobs offered by worker councils hiring, and apply wherever they want. But isn't this just a labor market?

In some ways, yes it is. But in crucial ways, it is not. It is like a labor market because everyone is free to apply for work wherever they wish, and worker councils are free to hire whomever they wish from whoever applies. Proponents of participatory economics make no apologies for this, because all this freedom is a good thing, and we would not have it any other way!

But it is not like a labor market in two important respects. First, in a capitalist labor market people are hired as employees, who must then do what they are told by those who own the enterprise – who are not them! In a participatory economy people are hired as members of worker councils with full and equal rights from the moment they arrive, not as employees. In other words, they work for themselves. This is also the case in models of worker self-managed market socialism where there are no employees, only members of worker councils. But in market socialism, like in capitalism, wage rates for members of worker councils are determined by the laws of supply and demand for different kinds of labor. This is *not* the case in a participatory economy, which is the second important difference compared to economies with labor markets.

Because compensation is determined by committees of co-workers based on the efforts and sacrifices one makes during work, in a participatory economy wages are not—indeed cannot—be negotiated as part of the hiring process. This means that the process of matching people with jobs is not only different from capitalist labor markets but from labor markets in worker-self managed market socialist economies as well.

David Schweickart claims there are no labor markets in his model of market socialism[1] because (a) it is not employees

---

1   David Schweickart, *Against Capitalism* (Westview Press, 1996) and *After Capitalism* (Rowman & Littlefield, 2002).

who are hired, but members of worker councils, and (b) every worker council is "free" to set its wage rates as they choose. The first point is true, and if we define "labor market" as a market for employees, then clearly there is no labor market in worker self-managed market socialism by definition. However, to assert that wage rates for worker council members are not set by the laws of supply and demand in his and other models of market socialism is untrue and misleading. After all, one could as easily point out that every capitalist firm is "free" to set its wage rates as it chooses, but does that mean that the laws of supply and demand play no role in wage determination in capitalism? Hardly. Any capitalist who chose to offer a wage rate for a particular category of labor below the going rate determined by the laws of supply and demand would be unable to hire employees in that labor category. Similarly, any worker self-managed market socialist enterprise which chose to offer a wage rate for a particular category of labor below the going rate determined by the laws of supply and demand would be unable to hire any council member in that labor category. As long as compensation is negotiated at the time of hiring, if people are free to apply and employers free to choose from applicants, supply and demand will set wage rates for the most part, and it is misleading to pretend otherwise. In any case, in a participatory economy compensation is determined after the fact by committees of one's workmates on the basis of effort and sacrifice, not by the laws of supply and demand for different kinds of labor.

CHAPTER THIRTEEN

CONSUMPTION

Consumer Councils

Every individual, family, or living unit belongs to a neighborhood consumption council. Each neighborhood council belongs to a federation of neighborhood councils the size of a precinct. Each precinct federation belongs to a city ward, or rural county federation. Each ward belongs to a city consumption council, each city and county council belongs to a state council, and each state council belongs to the national federation of consumption councils. The major purpose for "nesting" consumer councils into ever larger federations is to allow for the fact that different kinds of consumption affect different numbers of people. Some decisions affect only local residents, while others affect all who live in a city, county, state, or the entire country. Failure to arrange for all those affected by consumption activities to participate in choosing them not only implies a loss of self-management, but, if the preferences of some who are affected by a choice are disregarded or misrepresented, it also implies a loss of efficiency as well.

One of the serious liabilities of market systems is their systematic failure to allow for expression of desires for social consumption on an equal footing with desires for private consumption. In fact, a precise way to describe what markets do is they minimize the transaction costs of a buyer and seller arranging a deal between them while maximizing the transaction costs of participation for all those other than the buyer and seller who will be affected by the deal struck, usually to the point of disenfranchising them altogether.

In the participatory planning procedure described next chapter every neighborhood consumption council, and every federation of consumption councils submits proposals for what they want to consume. Neighborhood consumption councils aggregate the approved individual consumption requests of all households in the neighborhood, append requests for whatever neighborhood public goods they want, and submit the total list as the neighborhood consumption council's request in the planning process. Higher level federations of consumer councils simply request whatever public goods are consumed by all those who comprise their membership. Having different levels of consumer federations participate on an equal footing with neighborhood councils in the planning procedure eliminates any bias against collective consumption and in favor of individual consumption in a participatory economy.

Consumption Allowances

As explained last chapter, members of the labor force earn consumption rights based on their effort and sacrifice at work, as judged by their co-workers.[1] Those who are not expected to work because they are too young, still in school, disabled, or

---

1   It is important to note that in a participatory economy, while individuals earn consumption rights according to their work effort, users of scarce labor resources -- worker councils -- are charged *not* according to members' effort ratings but instead according to the opportunity costs of employing different kinds of labor, as explained next chapter. This allows us to pay people fairly and still make sure that when worker councils decide who to hire they do so based on the opportunity costs of using different kinds of labor, which is necessary to make sure scarce labor resources are allocated efficiently.

retired are also awarded consumption rights. How generous the consumption allowances of those excused from the workforce will be is decided democratically by society at large, as is the size of any consumption allowance for someone who is deemed able to work but declines to do so.

A household has a right to consume an amount which costs society an amount equal to the sum of the consumption allowances of all its members. The social cost of consumption requests is calculated by multiplying the amount of any good or service times the estimate of its social cost, which emerges from the participatory planning procedure as explained next chapter. Allowances aside, an individual's overall consumption is constrained in a participatory economy by her effort or sacrifice in work, just as an individual's overall consumption is constrained in a capitalist economy, by her income, which is usually *not* the same as her effort or sacrifice since most people's income in capitalism is less than their efforts warrant, while the income of a minority greatly exceeds what their efforts warrant.

There is complete freedom of choice in a participatory economy regarding *what* one wishes to consume. Moreover, consumer preferences determine what will be produced in a participatory economy whereas they only do so very imperfectly in market economies. Since markets bias consumer choice by overcharging for goods whose production or consumption entail positive external effects, undercharging for goods with negative external effects, and over supplying private goods relative to public goods, markets influence what will be produced in systematic ways that deviate from consumers' true preferences. Participatory planning is carefully designed to eliminate these biases which both infringe on "consumer sovereignty" and generate inefficiencies.

People in households consume public as well as private goods. For example, if a neighborhood consumption council requests a new swing set for its park each neighborhood resident is assessed his or her share of the social cost of the swing set. Likewise, if the city federation of consumer councils builds a new extension to its mass transit system, each city resident is assessed his or her share of the social cost of extending the line. In this way peoples' shares of the cost of all public goods requested by consumer councils and federations of which they are members are subtracted from their individual consumption allowance, and it is the remainder of their allowance that is available to cover their individual consumption requests.

What share of the costs of providing public goods different members of consumption councils and federations should pay can be left up to those councils and federation to decide. However, since a participatory economy goes to great lengths to make consumption allowances fair, and since public goods, by definition, are consumed by all, one can make a strong case for shares that are proportionate. For example, if there are 1000 members of my neighborhood consumption council each of us would be assessed one thousandth of the cost of a swing set for our neighborhood park.[2]

---

2   Where there is an easy, objective way to determine when some benefit more than others from a public good, consumer councils and federations may wish to deviate from assessments as proportionate shares. For example, paying for some public goods through user fees rather than general tax revenues may sometimes be reasonable. Even when there is no "objective" way to know who benefits more or less from a public good, councils and federations may want to experiment with some theoretical "demand revealing mechanisms" pioneered by T. Groves, J. Ledyard, E. Clark and others in the 1970s which succeed in charging those who truly do benefit more higher taxes without creating perverse incentives for everyone to pretend they benefit less than they actually do. The ingenious insight was to base individual's assessments not on their own reported willingness to pay, but instead on the reported willingness to pay of others. However, proponents of participatory economics happily leave choice of how to calculate assessments for public goods to consumer councils and federations as they see fit, and simply note that proportionate shares are not only easy, but have a long and honorable history, and are also what economists

Saving, Borrowing, and Special Needs

Anyone can save by consuming less than her consumption allowance for the year, deferring the remainder for later use. Borrowing, however, raises the issue of credibility. As long as someone who wishes to consume more this year than her consumption allowance warrants can be trusted to pay society back by consuming less than her allowance warrants in the future, there is no problem. In these normal cases borrowing is as simple and straightforward as saving. However, what if a person borrows year after year, and in amounts that cast doubt on her ability to pay society back all she owes? In capitalism loan officers in banks – or those who approve credit limits on credit cards – make these judgment calls. In a participatory economy we leave monitoring the credibility of personal loan requests up to neighborhood consumption councils since they are also in charge of aggregating household consumption requests, reviewing special need requests, and handling adjustments to consumption requests throughout the year.

It also makes sense for neighborhood consumption councils to decide when to grant members extra consumption allowances due to special needs. Remember that those excused from work for any reason already will have consumption allowances as determined by society as a whole. And even those who can work but choose not to may well have some allowance. For the vast majority of public goods there will also be no charge, which presumably includes things like medical expenses, as in Cuba where for the past fifty years all medical services have been dispensed free of charge as needed. So all we are talking about here are truly unforeseeable special needs that sometimes do arise. Neighborhood consumption councils are free to grant extra consumption allowances to members in special need as the council sees fit. Unless the neighborhood council makes a special appeal to higher level consumer federations for others to bear part of the cost of any special need requests the council

call "incentive compatible."

grants during the planning procedure, then special needs grants are effectively being paid for out of the allowances of everyone else in the neighborhood council.

Should there be an interest rate paid on personal savings and charged on personal loans? Without reviewing a lengthy literature on this subject we can give a simple answer. There would be little harm done if no interest were paid or charged on personal savings and loans. And since this is delightfully simple it may well be the best choice. However, there would also be nothing wrong with paying a rate of interest equal to the annual rate of increase in per capita economic well-being, and charging this same rate of interest on personal loans, perhaps with a small "risk premium" sufficient to cover actual losses from loans consumers default on.[3]

Deciding What I Want… and Changing My Mind

A participatory economy is a planned economy. This means we must have some idea what people want to consume in order to formulate a plan for how to produce it. In market economies consumers do not "pre-order," and instead producers are left to guess what consumers will eventually demand. Not only do corporations expend a great deal of resources trying to estimate (and influence!) what people will want to buy, the extent to which they guess wrong generates market disequilibria and what economists call "false trading" while market prices adjust – all of which generates inefficiency. Of course those who want us to believe markets are God's gift to the human species don't go out of their way to remind us that when markets are out of equilibrium inefficiency is always the result. However, simply

---

3   It is important to note that investments by worker councils to expand and improve their productive capacities are decided during the investment planning process described in chapter 16, and these investments are *not* financed out of personal savings. So the rate of interest we are discussing here is merely a payment by those who want to consume earlier to consumers willing to consume later.

reading the necessary assumptions behind the fundamental theorems of mainstream economics "high theory" makes this quite clear to any who care to notice. In other words, the convenience for consumers of never having to pre-order in market economies is actually bought at the expense of a significant amount of economic inefficiency as resources are wasted producing more of some goods and less of others than it turns out people want. Not to speak of the waste during economic slumps like the current Great Recession when a significant proportion of global productive resources sit idle altogether, not because people don't want the goods and services they would produce, but because producers guess correctly there will be insufficient "effective demand" to buy them.

A participatory economy provides a remarkably cheap way to mobilize as much information about what consumers will want as possible to avoid all this "macro" inefficiency that plagues market economies. Neighborhood consumption councils and consumer federations make consumption desires known (for both private and public goods) during the participatory planning process by entering proposals on behalf of their members.

However, neighborhood proposals for private consumption are really just neighborhood-wide best guesses. In other words, nobody is going to hold households to their consumption requests when it turns out they want to consume more of some things and less of others than they pre-ordered. We simply ask households to place a pre-order so neighborhood consumption councils can participate in the planning process as described next chapter. What we envision is consumers spending a couple of hours of their time going over their consumption from the previous year and making adjustments up and down where they think they will want to. That is less time than it takes the average person to prepare her tax returns every year.

We are well aware that consumers will misestimate what they ask for and need to make changes during the year, and that some consumers will prove more reliable and others more fickle. As a matter of fact, being quite lazy about such matters, I would not bother to update my consumption proposal at all! And being very irresponsible about communication I would also, in all likelihood, fail to respond to the prompt from my neighborhood consumption council reminding me to send in a new proposal for the coming year. I would simply allow my neighborhood council to re-enter what their records show I actually ended up consuming last year as my pre-order again for this year. Sound difficult?

The easiest way to think about this is to imagine each consumer with a swipe card that records what they consume during the year as they pick it up, and compares their rate of consumption for items against the amount they had asked for. If one's rate of consumption for an item deviates by say 20% from the rate implied by the annual request, consumers could be "prompted" and asked if they want to make a change. If at the end of the year the total social cost of someone's actual consumption differs from the social cost of what they had asked, and been approved for, they would simply be credited or debited appropriately in their savings account.

One of the functions of consumer councils and federations is to coordinate changes in consumption among themselves. If another consumer wants more of an item I pre-ordered but no longer want, there is no need to change the amount the agreed upon production plan called for. Whenever consumer councils and federations (which will function like clearing houses for adjustments) discover that changes do not cancel out, the national consumer federation will have to discuss adjustments with industry federations of worker councils. Computerized inventory management systems and "real time" supply chains are already fixtures in the global economy, which makes adjustments much smoother than they would have been only a few decades ago.

In any case, to whatever extent consumers do foresee their needs, a participatory economy is positioned to capture the efficiency gains of planning over market disequilibria. To the extent that consumers cannot accurately gauge their desires, councils and federations will have to negotiate mid-course adjustments. But a participatory economy is certainly not powerless to respond to changes in consumer desires. Is it possible that some consumer may not receive some particular item exactly when they want it if it was not in their original order? Yes. But that should not occur often, and if memory serves, not every child found a Cabbage Patch Kid* under her tree the first Christmas those dolls became all the rage.

Consumer councils and federations also afford consumers much greater clout *vis a vis* producers over quality and defects than consumers have in market economies. Critics of participatory economics have mistakenly assumed it is no different from Soviet-style command planning in this regard. It is true consumers were even more disenfranchised in the centrally planned economies than they are in market economies. Soviet, Chinese, Cuban, and Polish consumers not only confronted a huge state distribution system alone, but faced a "take it or take nothing" proposition. In market economies individual consumers face powerful corporations which devote significant resources to manipulating us. The advantage is we can walk away from one corporate behemoth and buy from another (which mouths the double-speak mantra "the customer is always right" with equal insincerity). But in a participatory economy neighborhood consumer councils and federations put consumers on an even playing field with producers, *and* each consumer has freedom of exit. Instead of relying for information on shopping displays and advertisements from profit seeking producers, consumers in a participatory economy will surf websites and roam malls run by consumer federations responsible to them, and get product information from their consumer councils and federations rather than from producers.

It is the difference between getting information about the likelihood of washing machines breaking down from GE and Sears or from Consumer Reports. It is the difference between

GM having to hoodwink Robin Hahnel or Ralph Nader and his research associates about automobile safety. Worker councils don't get credited for goods returned. If a consumer is unsatisfied with a product she only has to refuse it and have it returned as unacceptable by her consumer council. Then the question of whether or not the product delivered was up to standards, and the producer deserves credit or not, is settled between the consumer council, or federation, and the worker council who made it, or their federation. Won't it be nice when all of us can hand over our customer complaints to a powerful player to take care of for us? Come to think of it, isn't that why the 1% always have lawyers on retainer?

CHAPTER FOURTEEN

PARTICIPATORY PLANNING

One needn't be an economist to think through the pros and cons of different systems of reward and organizing work and consumption. As a matter of fact, non-economists frequently exhibit more common sense about such matters than many trained economists. But when it comes to thinking about how best to coordinate the interrelated affairs of millions of different producers and consumers, non-economists often find themselves at a disadvantage. This chapter takes on a difficult job: explaining how participatory planning works in plain English so readers' eyes do not glaze over. We begin by reviewing the "challenges" we face when designing a desirable coordinating mechanism.

The Challenge

How can we empower worker and consumer councils while protecting the interests of others in the economy who are affected by what these councils do? How can we give groups of workers *user rights* over parts of *society's* productive resources without allowing them to benefit unfairly from productive resources that belong to, and should benefit everyone?

What socialists have long understood is that what any one group in an economy does will inevitably affect many others. The conclusion many socialists have drawn from this fact is that democratic planning must allow all to have a voice and say regarding all economic decisions. This, of course, is correct as far as it goes. But different decisions do not usually affect everyone to the same extent. One might call this the *fundamental dilemma* faced by those of us who want to organize a system of economic decision making that gives people decision making power *to the degree* they are affected by different economic decisions: Most economic decisions do affect many people, but to differing degrees. The challenge is how to give workers and consumers in their own councils a degree of autonomy over what they do that is appropriate.

Encouraging popular participation in economic decision making is hard. After all, those who actually do the work have been discouraged from participating in decision making ever since humans "ascended" from more egalitarian hunting and gathering societies to class systems with ruling elites. For the past three hundred years workers have been taught they are incapable of making important economic decisions, and to thank their lucky stars they have capitalist employers and managers to do their thinking for them. Developing a participatory culture that encourages those who have long been a silenced majority inside their workplaces to actively participate in deciding what they will produce and how they will produce it is difficult enough, even though these decisions have immediate and palpable impacts on workers' daily lives. Encouraging popular participation in coordinating the interrelated activities of millions of different workplaces and neighborhoods, and in investment and long-run development planning, where the relevance to one's personal life is more attenuated and less obvious, is even more difficult. Yet this is the historical legacy of capitalist alienation we must overcome.

Moreover, the price of failure is monstrous. Biologists teach us that nature abhors an ecological vacuum, by which they mean that in complex ecological systems any empty niche will quickly be filled by some organism or another. If there is a single lesson we should learn from human history it is that society abhors a power vacuum. If people do not control their own lives then someone else will. And if there is a single lesson we should learn from the history of twentieth century Communist economies it is that if workers and consumers do not run the economy themselves, then some economic elite will rise to do it for them.

How can we give workers and consumers in their councils the autonomy necessary to stimulate them to become and remain active participants in economic decision making while ensuring that worker and consumer councils do not make choices that are socially irresponsible? How is it possible to grant small groups of workers and consumers enough autonomy to encourage them to put time and effort into participating without disenfranchising others who are affected by the decisions they make, even though it be to a lesser extent? How can we grant groups of workers the right to use some of society's productive resources as they would like without allowing them to benefit unfairly from doing so? How can we convince ordinary workers and consumers who have been discouraged in every conceivable way from trying to participate in economic decision making that things will now be different, and participation will finally be worthwhile? The participatory planning procedure was designed to answer these challenges.

The Planning Procedure

Conceptually participatory planning is quite simple: The participants in the planning procedure are worker councils and federations, consumer councils and federations, and an Iteration Facilitation Board (IFB), which plays a perfunctory role. The procedure works as follows: (1) At the beginning of each round the IFB announces current estimates of the opportunity costs of all natural resources, categories of labor, and capital stocks, current estimates of the social cost of producing different goods and services, and current estimates of the damage caused by emissions of different pollutants. These estimates can be thought of as "indicative prices" since they provide useful "indications" of what it costs society when we use different primary resources and emit different pollutants, and what it costs society to produce different goods and services. (2) Consumer councils and federations respond by making consumption proposals. That is, they propose what goods and services they want to consume and what levels of emissions of pollutants that affect them they are willing to tolerate. Worker councils respond by making production proposals. That is, they propose what "outputs" they want to produce (not only the useful goods and services they would provide but also any emissions of pollutants), and the "inputs" they want to use to accomplish this (including not only intermediate goods they need from other worker councils but any natural resources, capital goods, and different kinds of labor they would need as well). (3) The IFB adds up all the requests to use, and offers to supply each natural resource, each category of labor, each kind of capital good, and each pollutant, and adjusts its estimate of the opportunity or social cost of the good up or down in proportion to the degree of excess demand or supply for that good. These three steps are repeated in subsequent rounds, or "iterations" until there is no longer any excess demand for any final or intermediate good, natural resource, category of labor, capital stock, or permission to emit any pollutant.

Each round in this social, iterative procedure begins with new, more accurate estimates of opportunity and social costs, followed by revised proposals from all councils and federations in light of new information about how their desires affect others. Each council and federation must revise and resubmit its own proposal until it meets with approval from the other councils and federations. The planning procedure continues to subsequent rounds until a "feasible," comprehensive plan for the year is reached, i.e. a plan where everything someone is counting on will actually be available.

Consumption council and federation proposals are evaluated by multiplying the quantity of every good or service requested by the estimated social cost of producing a unit of the good or service, to be compared to the average effort rating plus allowances of the members of the consumption council or federation requesting the goods and services. If, for example, the average effort rating plus allowances for a neighborhood consumption council is equal to the social average, this should entitle them to consume goods and services whose production costs society an amount equal to the average cost of providing a neighborhood consumption request. A neighborhood council with higher than average effort ratings plus allowances (indicating that they had made greater than average sacrifices as workers) is presumably entitled to a consumption bundle which cost society more than the average; a neighborhood council with lower than average effort ratings plus allowances should presumably only be entitled to a consumption bundle which cost less than the average.

The important point is that the estimates of opportunity and social costs generated during the planning procedure make it easy to calculate the social cost of consumption requests. This is important information for councils and federations making consumption requests since otherwise they have no way of knowing the extent to which they are asking others to bear burdens on their behalf. It is also important for councils and federations which must vote to approve or disapprove consumption requests of others, since otherwise they have no way of knowing if a request is fair (consistent with sacrifices those making the request have made) or unfair (in excess of sacrifices made).

Production proposals are evaluated by comparing the estimated social benefits of outputs to the estimated social cost of inputs. In any round of the planning procedure the social benefits of a production proposal are calculated simply by multiplying quantities of proposed outputs by their "indicative" prices—including negative prices for proposed emissions of pollutants and summing, and social costs of a production proposal are calculated by multiplying inputs requested by their "indicative" prices and summing. If the social benefits exceed the social costs—that is, if the *social benefit to cost ratio* of a production proposal exceeds one— everyone else is presumably made better off by allowing the worker council to do what they have proposed. On the other hand, if the social benefit to cost ratio is less than one, the rest of society would presumably be worse off if the workers go ahead and do what they have proposed, unless there is something "the numbers" fail to capture. Again, the "indicative" prices make it easy to calculate the social benefit to cost ratio for any production proposal, allowing worker councils making proposals to determine if their own proposals are socially responsible, and giving all councils who must vote to approve or disapprove production proposals of others an easy way to assess whether those proposals are socially responsible.

This procedure "whittles down" overly ambitious proposals submitted by worker and consumer councils about what they would like to do to a "feasible" plan where everything someone is expecting to be able to use will actually be available. Consumers requesting more than their effort ratings and allowances warrant are forced to either reduce the amounts they request, or shift their requests to less socially costly items if they expect to win the approval of other councils who have no reason to approve consumption requests whose social costs are not justified by the sacrifices of those making them. Similarly, worker councils are forced to either increase their efforts, shift toward producing a more desirable mix of outputs, or shift to a less costly mix of inputs to win approval for their proposals from other councils who have no reason to approve production proposals whose social costs exceed their social benefits. Efficiency is promoted as consumers and workers attempt to shift their proposals in response to updated information about opportunity and social costs in order to avoid reductions in consumption or increases in work effort. Equity is promoted when further shifting is insufficient to win approval from fellow consumers and workers which can eventually only be achieved through consumption reduction or greater work effort. As iterations proceed, consumption and production proposals move closer to mutual feasibility, and estimates more closely approximate true opportunity and social costs as the procedure generates equity and efficiency simultaneously. Admittedly, that is a lot to digest, and there are important technical issues of concern to economists not treated here. In this regard it has been demonstrated that the participatory procedure outlined above will reach a feasible plan that is a Pareto optimum under less restrictive assumptions than those necessary to prove that the general equilibrium of a private enterprise, market economy will do so. In particular, participatory planning accommodates externalities and public goods efficiently whereas market economies do not.[1] But this is what it boils down to:

When worker councils make proposals they are asking permission to use particular parts of the productive resources that belong to everyone. In effect their proposals say: "If the rest of you, with whom we are engaged in a cooperative division of labor, agree to allow us to use productive resources belonging to all of us as inputs, then we promise to deliver the following goods and services as outputs for others to use." When consumer councils make proposals they are asking permission to consume goods and services whose production entails social costs. In effect their proposals say: "We believe the effort ratings we received from our co-workers, together with allowances members of households have been granted, indicate that we deserve the right to consume goods and services whose production entails an equivalent level of social costs."

The planning procedure is designed to make it clear when a worker council production proposal is inefficient and when a consumption council proposal is unfair, and allows other worker and consumer councils to deny approval for proposals when they seem to be inefficient or unfair. But initial self-ac-

1   Readers interested in these technical issues should see chapter 5 in Albert and Hahnel, *The Political Economy of Participatory Economics* (Princeton UP, 1991), "Socialism As It Was Always Meant to Be," *Review of Radical Political Economics (24, 3&4)*, Fall and Winter 1992: 46-66, and "Participatory Planning," *Science & Society (56, 1)*, Spring 1992: 39-59.

tivity proposals, and all revisions of proposals, are entirely up to each worker and consumer council itself. In other words, if a worker council production proposal or neighborhood council consumption proposal is not approved, the council that made the proposal (nobody else) can revise its proposal for resubmission in the next round of the planning procedure. This aspect of the participatory planning procedure distinguishes it from all other planning models, which advocates believe is crucial if workers and consumers are to enjoy meaningful self-management.

Participatory Planning and Self-Management

Verifying that a planning procedure will promote efficient use of productive resources is of great concern to economists. However, citizens and activists should be more concerned with whether or not a planning procedure promotes popular participation in economic decision making, and it is in this regard that advocates believe participatory planning most outshines other versions of democratic planning.

Of course a participatory economy cannot give every person decision making authority *exactly* to the degree they are affected in every decision that is made. Instead the idea is to devise procedures that *approximate* this goal. How does a participatory economy do this? (1) Every worker has one vote in his or her worker council. (2) In large worker councils subunits can govern their own internal affairs. (3) Consumers are free to consume whatever kinds of goods and services they prefer as long as their effort rating or allowance is sufficient to cover the overall cost to society of producing the goods and services they request. (4) Consumers each have one vote in her neighborhood consumption council regarding the level and composition of neighborhood public good consumption. (5) Federations responsible for different levels of collective consumption and limiting pollution levels are also governed by democratic decision making procedures where each council in the federation sends representatives to the federation in proportion to the size of its membership. *But most importantly, in the participatory planning procedure (6) worker and consumer councils and federations not only propose what they, themselves, will do in the initial round of the participatory planning procedure, they alone make all revisions regarding their own activity during subsequent rounds.*

Does all this guarantee that if a decision affects me 1.13 times as much as it affects someone else, I will have exactly 1.13 more say than they do? Of course not. But I will get to decide what kinds of private goods I consume; my neighbors and I will get to decide what local public goods we consume; all who use larger level public goods will get to decide what those will be, as long as our work efforts and sacrifices warrant the social expense of providing us with what we want. My co-workers and I will get to decide what we produce and how we produce it, as long as we propose to use society's scarce productive resources efficiently.

Who Says "No"?

Who decides if proposals from worker and consumer councils and federations are acceptable? In central planning this decision resides with the central planning authority. The justification given for this is that only a central planning authority can gather the necessary information and wield sufficient computational power to determine if proposals would use scarce productive resources efficiently and distribute economic burdens and benefits fairly. In other words, it is presumed that a central planning authority, and only a central authority, can protect the social interest. But leaving aside the more general question of whether or not any authority can be trusted to protect any interest other than its own, it turns out on careful examination that both parts of the traditional rationale for giving central planners power to approve or disapprove work proposals are false. A central planning authority cannot gather the necessary information to make competent decisions, while it *is* possible to provide ordinary workers and consumers in their councils with the necessary information for them to do so by using the participatory planning procedure.

Because a great deal of information about what different worker councils can and cannot do resides with those who work there, and because under central planning there are perverse incentives that lead workplaces to mislead central planners about their true capabilities, it is so difficult and costly for central planning authorities to acquire accurate information that it is naive to assume they will be able to do so. This problem, known as the "tacit knowledge" critique of central planning, is now widely acknowledged. What is generally not understood is that a different kind of planning procedure can eliminate these and other perverse incentives and thereby provide everyone with accurate information necessary to make informed judgments.

In the participatory planning procedure worker councils would only harm themselves by failing to make proposals that accurately reveal their true capabilities because underestimating their capabilities lowers the likelihood of being allocated the productive resources they want. As discussed in more detail in chapter 17, the participatory planning procedure also eliminates perverse incentives regarding pollution that are endemic to market systems. Under participatory planning it is in the best interests of pollution victims to reveal how much they are truly affected by pollution, and these negative effects are fully accounted for in the social costs of producing different goods and services. Neither is true in market economies. Finally, in the participatory planning procedure, requests for different levels of public goods are treated simultaneously and in the same way as requests for private goods and services, whereas markets create a bias in favor of individual consumption requests at the expense of collective consumption.

By eliminating perverse incentives endemic to central planning and markets the participatory planning procedure is able to generate estimates of the opportunity costs of scarce productive resources, the social costs of harmful emissions, and the social costs of producing goods and services that are as accurate as can be hoped for. But this means participatory planning generates the necessary information to make informed judgments about work and consumption proposals. *Everyone* has the information necessary to calculate the social benefit to cost ratios of *every* worker council proposal, and *everyone* has the information necessary to compare the social cost of *every* consumer council to the average effort rating of its members.

This means that allowing councils to vote "yea" or "nay" on the proposals of other councils does not entail time-consuming evaluation of proposals. All they have to do is look at the social benefit-to-cost ratio for proposals from worker councils. When the ratio is below average it means the worker council is *probably* using resources inefficiently or not working as hard as others. Similarly, when the social cost per member of a consumer council proposal is higher than the average effort rating plus allowances of its members, they are *probably* being too greedy and unfair to others. But otherwise, everyone else is better off approving a proposal from a worker council, and otherwise a proposal from a consumer council is perfectly fair. Of course there will be exceptions to these rules and it is important to design appeals procedures federations can use to handle unusual cases where "the numbers lie." But most proposals can be voted up or down very quickly because the participatory planning procedure makes it possible for each council to judge whether or not the proposals of other councils are socially responsible without wasting time. This procedure also creates incentives to approve socially responsible proposals and only disapprove proposals that are inefficient or unfair.

Members of worker councils will have to meet to discuss and decide what they want to propose to produce and what inputs they want to request. But participation in these meetings is part of people's job, not something they do after hours. Members of neighborhood consumption councils will have to meet to discuss what neighborhood public goods they want to ask for. Representatives from councils that comprise a federation of consumer councils will have to meet to discuss what public goods larger groups of consumers want to request. However, these are all meetings *within* worker and consumer councils and *within* federations, not meetings *between* councils and federations. Moreover, these meetings are only concerned with what the councils or federations want to do themselves. The discussion is not about what people think the overall, comprehensive plan for the economy should be. In other words, discussions are about what we might call "self-activity" proposals.

Dangers to Avoid

Authoritarian planning discourages worker and consumer participation because it disenfranchises them. Poorly designed systems of democratic planning might continue to discourage worker and consumer participation in a different way. If worker and consumer councils have no autonomous area of action regarding their own work and consumption activities, but must submit to seemingly endless discussion, debate, and negotiations about what they want to do with many others, in many different planning bodies, through representatives, ordinary workers and consumers may well lapse back into apathy even if there is no authoritarian planning procedure to disenfranchise them.

There is a serious danger that some forms of democratic planning can discourage participation on the part of ordinary workers and consumers by requiring them to engage in too much negotiation with others, especially if most of these negotiations are conducted by representatives. In this case, ordinary workers and consumers would no longer be disenfranchised as they are under authoritarian planning, but if procedures for involving all who are affected are cumbersome and clumsy, and if those procedures rely primarily on representatives, they may become a practical barrier to participation that only the most dedicated and determined workers and consumers will be willing to fight through. In other words, when poorly organized, democratic planning can become just another bureaucratic maze from the perspective of ordinary workers and consumers, leading to what economist Nancy Folbre has warned could become a "dictatorship of the sociable."

Participatory planning is designed so worker and consumer councils can decide what they want to do as long as it does not misuse productive resources that belong to all, or take unfair advantage of others. It is designed to help worker and consumer councils demonstrate to one another that their proposals are socially responsible by generating the information to form such judgments. It is designed to avoid unproductive and contentious meetings where representatives from different councils make proposals not only about what those they represent will do, but about what workers in other councils will do as well. The planning procedure may take a number of rounds before proposals are confirmed as fair and not wasteful of social resources, and before excess demands are eliminated and a feasible plan is reached. But rounds in the planning procedure are *not* rounds of increasingly contentious meetings between representatives from different councils to debate the merits of different, overall, national production plans without information necessary to make informed decisions. Instead they are meetings *inside* each worker and consumer council and federation to reconsider and revise its *own* proposal about what the members of each council want to do themselves, with clear guidelines about what will win approval from others. Unlike other models of democratic planning: (1) councils never have to argue over someone else's ideas about what they should do; (2) only in rare and special circumstances do councils have to plead their case for what they want to do in meetings with others; and (3) there is always a clear agenda for any meetings required to adjudicate special appeals.

In short, the goal is to arrive at an economic plan through deliberative democracy. But deliberation can take two very different forms. Deliberation can be over competing comprehensive annual plans, and take place at meetings attended by only a few representatives from each council. Or, deliberation can be over what each worker and consumer council wants to do itself, and take place within each worker and consumer council among all members to formulate and revise their "self-activity" proposal in response to feedback from others and more accurate estimates of opportunity and social costs. The differences between these two ways to carry out deliberative democracy are crucial. While the first conception of deliberative democracy may be more common, it has three disadvantages: (1) Only a few people from each council benefit from the deliberations (those sent as representatives) who then bear the burden of trying to convey their deliberative experience to those they represent. (2) Members of a worker council never formulate proposals for what they want to do. Instead their representatives, together with representatives from other councils formulate proposals about what everyone, including them, will do. (3) Meetings of representatives proposing different comprehensive economic plans do not generate quantitative estimates of opportunity and social costs, without which sensible discussion of the merits of different proposals and plans is severely hampered, if not impossible. The participatory planning procedure, on the other hand, empowers ordinary workers and consumers, not merely their representatives, to formulate their own work and consumption proposals, and generates estimates of opportunity and social costs that are as accurate as can be hoped for.

Unfortunately, the importance of procedures that can be relied on to generate reasonably accurate information necessary for making informed social choices is often lost on activists who have little or no economic training. While an aversion to putting prices on things is understandable in the context of capitalism which, in the words of Oscar Wilde, "knows the price of everything and the value of nothing," unfortunately without reasonably accurate estimates of opportunity and social costs it is impossible for ordinary people to participate in planning sensibly. If we want ordinary people to participate we must not only give them voice and vote in our planning procedures, we must also give them easy access to the essential information they need to arrive at sensible decisions quickly.

Unless I know the opportunity costs of resources a work proposal requires, unless I know the social costs of producing the intermediate inputs needed, and unless I can compare these costs to the social benefits of the outputs the workers propose to deliver, how can I sensibly decide if a work proposal is socially responsible? If it is a work proposal my workmates and I are preparing, I need to know this in order to be able to ascertain whether we are proposing to do something that is socially responsible or irresponsible. I also need to know this to determine whether our work proposal will be quickly approved by others, or is likely to be turned down pending special appeals we would have to go through. If the work proposal is one that another worker council has proposed I need to know this to figure out whether I want to vote "yea" or "nay", which I will want to do very quickly in most cases. Without reasonably accurate estimates of opportunity and social costs there is no way to make these judgment calls. On the other hand, with this information necessary calculations can be done quickly, results can be made immediately available to everyone, and ordinary people can rapidly make all necessary decisions in each round of the planning procedure.

CHAPTER FIFTEEN
INCENTIVES

Throughout history many people have chosen to behave in ways they deemed to be in the social interest despite the fact that they had good reason to believe their behavior was contrary to their own, personal, self-interest. Moreover, recent research in evolutionary biology and evolutionary game theory suggest that not only have successful societies developed social norms to induce such behavior, but there is every reason to believe natural selection would have favored genetic dispositions toward behavior that helped the group, not just the individual, survive.

However, it is highly unlikely that natural selection failed to reward what we should think of as a "healthy self-regard" in a species capable of purposeful action. Moreover, any dispassionate review of human history would be hard pressed to deny that people often *do* act according to their perceptions of what serves their self-interest. While social norms and circumstances can greatly affect the degree to which people will favor self-interest over social-interest when the two are in conflict, we should not see our goal as eliminating self-interest through rhetorical appeal and social pressure.

The question is not if people serve the social interest *or* their self interest. Humans are genetically programmed to serve *both* the social interest *and* their self-interest, and it is unrealistic to believe that a significant portion of the body politic will behave in ways they have good reason to believe are contrary to their self-interest, no matter how strong calls for self-sacrifice may be. People do have a regard for the social interest, and *all things being equal* there is good reason to believe we can rely on most people to act in the social interest. But it is quite another thing to expect people to serve the social interest when they must do so to the detriment of their own personal well-being. So our job is to find ways to no longer put people in this quandary. If we want socially responsible behavior, then we must design an economy that no longer punishes people who behave in socially responsible ways and rewards people for behaving in socially irresponsible ways.

Fairness, Trust, and Solidarity

A participatory economy is designed to eliminate conflicts between social and self-interest. This does not mean proponents of a participatory economy do not value solidarity, and measure social progress by its growth. But we see solidarity as a product of people's historical experience. Too often people could not trust others to treat them fairly, or behave in socially responsible ways. Only when there is a new track record of people being treated fairly do we expect people to overcome their historic mistrust of one another. Trust is a prerequisite for solidarity, and trust must be earned. Yes, increasing solidarity is perhaps the most important measure of social progress, but it will be strengthened primarily by creating a different historical legacy, rather than exhortation or heroic example by a faithful few, and the different historical legacy will be created by eliminating the conflict between social and self-interest, not by eliminating people's self-regard. How does a participatory economy eliminate the conflict between social and self-interest? What follows is a brief review of what has already been covered regarding motivational and allocative efficiency, followed by some brief remarks on incentives and dynamic efficiency.

Incentives in a Participatory Economy

Motivational Efficiency: As explained, workers are compensated according to personal sacrifice, or work effort in a participatory economy because this is just and fair. One's effort and sacrifice are assessed by co-workers because as problematic as this may be any other system of evaluation would be far worse.

In truth, economic productivity is largely the result of scientific and technological knowledge accumulated over decades and centuries, embodied in equipment and organizations of work that are also inherited. What any one of us could produce absent this "gift" from the past, and absent the cooperation of others, is miniscule compared to what we can produce, on average, by using this gift together. What is absurd is the notion that some deserve to appropriate thousands of times more than others from the bounty this public good of social economic productivity provides. When we understand that each generation inherits its productive potential it is easier to see why only differences in the efforts and sacrifices people make when setting this productive potential in motion should serve as the basis for any differences in rewards. In any case, while the quantity and quality of non-labor inputs one has to work with, how many others there are in one's occupation, talent, and luck all influence how productive people's work will be, the only factor over which people have any control is how much effort they exert. So not only is rewarding effort the fair thing to do, it is also the best way to motivate people to perform up to their abilities. In sum, rewarding effort as judged by workmates aligns individual interest with the social interest quite nicely, particularly when "effort" includes any above average sacrifices incurred in education and training.

Allocative Efficiency: It is in the self-interest of individual worker councils to have more and higher quality inputs to work with, while it is in the social interest to allocate scarce productive resources to wherever they are most socially valuable. Particularly in light of the fact that only a worker council can propose and revise its requests for inputs, how does the planning procedure reconcile the self-interest of worker councils with the social interest?

As already explained, in the participatory planning process worker councils are asking others' permission to be allowed to use scarce productive resources that belong to everyone, as well as products and services others must produce, in exchange for a promise to deliver certain amounts of socially valuable goods and services. Since the planning procedure generates ever more accurate estimates of social costs and benefits, it is easy to see if the social benefits expected from the outputs a worker council promises to deliver exceed the social costs of the inputs it is requesting. Only in this case is it in the interest of all the other worker and consumer councils to vote to approve the proposal. So in order to obtain the resources they want to work with, i.e. in order to serve their own interests, worker councils are required to serve the social interest as well.

Dynamic Efficiency: Only with regard to rewarding innovation is there a possible conflict between two different aspects of the social interest in a participatory economy- what economists call dynamic and static efficiency. To achieve static efficiency, all productive innovations will be made available immediately to all workplaces, which have every incentive to put them to good use. If innovations were produced as "outputs" in industry and consumer federation research and development units, where workers are rewarded for their efforts toward developing innovations, there is no conflict between static and dynamic efficiency. And since R&D is a public good, and a participatory economy tends to allocate more resources toward the production of public goods than market economies, this should increase the pace of innovation. However, since innovations are shared with all immediately, where is the incentive for individual worker councils to innovate rather than wait for special R&D units or other worker councils to do so? In particular, will it prove desirable to provide material rewards to innovating workplaces, above and beyond what their members' sacrifices entitle them to?

There is good reason to believe in an economy where it is unlikely that status will be achieved through conspicuous consumption, and where social serviceability will be more highly esteemed, that rewarding workers in highly innovative enterprises with consumption rights in excess of sacrifices may not be necessary. However, if people in a participatory economy come to the conclusion that extra rewards for workers in innovating enterprises are needed, any such rewards will be determined democratically by all citizens. However, unlike patents which provide material rewards for innovation in private enterprise economies by prohibiting others from using the innovation, which generates a great deal of "static" inefficiency, any material rewards for innovating enterprises will not limit their use by others.

Tying Up Loose Ends

There are two issues that need to be addressed, and this is as good a place as any to do it. How are enterprises born, and how do they die in a participatory economy? What are the pros and cons of capping average effort ratings for worker councils in different ways?

Enterprises die, and their members must search for work elsewhere, when a worker council fails to make a proposal approved by others during the participatory planning procedure. This may seem harsh at first, but this "discipline" is necessary to ensure that scarce productive resources are not misused. If a worker council cannot come up with a proposal whose social benefit to cost ratio is at least one, this means that others can use the productive resources they are asking for, which belong to everyone, more efficiently than they can. Since we don't want resources used less efficiently than they could be, we should disband worker councils who cannot use them as efficiently as others.

However, there may be situations where "the numbers lie," and a worker council whose proposal has a social benefit to cost ratio less than one is actually not using resources inefficiently. This is why we need appeal procedures, which should ordinarily be conducted by the industry federation a worker council belongs to.

Moreover, any council in danger of being disbanded should be provided help by their industry federation. After all, there must be some reason a particular group of workers are not coming up with proposals to use resources as effectively as other groups of workers in their industry. Before disbanding the council and sending their members to work elsewhere permanently, some workers from the council in danger of being disbanded should be sent as guest workers in more successful worker councils in the industry to see how they are doing things, and the industry federation should send members from successful councils to consult and work as guest workers in the council in trouble. Sometimes this will prevent the need to disband a worker council.

But what happens when all efforts to correct what is wrong fail, and a worker council must be disbanded? Does this mean its members must suffer personally? Since the annual production plan provides for full employment, there will be jobs for them in more successful worker councils, if not in their own industry in others. Moreover, their expected income working elsewhere should be as high, or higher than it was in the council that was disbanded. And finally, a participatory economy can and should provide the kind of generous stipends for retraining and relocation provided by labor market boards to laid off workers in Sweden and Norway during the heydays of social democracy in Scandinavia during the 1970s.

Notice there is no issue of selling off enterprise assets when a worker council is disbanded in a participatory economy. Worker councils do not "own" the resources they use in the first place. They only have "user rights" premised on the assumption that they were making efficient use of social resources. So any factory buildings, machines, or inventory stocks in the possession of a council that is disbanded are simply reallocated through the participatory planning procedure to enterprises whose bids to use them are accepted in the next annual planning procedure.

How are new enterprises born in a participatory economy? In capitalism, any enterprising group of people can start up a company. In a participatory economy, any enterprising group of people can start up a new worker council. In capitalism entrepreneurs put up the money needed to start an enterprise. In a participatory economy new worker councils bid for the resources they need to get started in the participatory planning process. If they submit a proposal that is accepted, they're good to go. Otherwise not. They do not put up any money of their own, nor do they enjoy any rights or privileges beyond the rights and privileges of any other members of the worker council who are hired later. What we might call the entrepreneurial group has no extra financial risk and receives no extra compensation. They simply enjoy the benefits of starting a new worker council with others they like and agree with.

But in the real world the actual birthing process for new enterprises is more complicated. Banks, bond, and stock markets are the midwives for new corporations in capitalism. Even the smallest new business requires a bank loan, or line of credit, to get started. But not only must loan officers deem a business proposal sufficiently promising to provide startup loans, to grow small companies require the services of banks to manage "public offerings" to sell bonds and shares of stock in the fledgling enterprise.

In a real world participatory economy, industry federations serve as midwives for new worker councils. First of all, it is industry federations who know how much expansion has been authorized for the industry as a whole by the investment plan. Industry expansion can be handled by increasing output in existing worker councils, creating new worker councils, or both. But just as banks judge the "credibility" of new entrepreneur's business plans in capitalism, industry federations judge whether or not a group who has proposed to form a new worker council are "credible." The industry federation will need to check to make sure the people involved do not have a track record of starting worker councils, getting proposals accepted during the planning procedure, only to fail to deliver what they promised. Presumably the industry federation will also make sure at least some in the group have the requisite training and experience. So in real world participatory economies groups who want to start up a new worker council will apply to the appropriate industry federation to be certified as "credible," after which they can participate in the planning procedure and try to acquire the resources they need.

How should average effort ratings in worker councils be capped? As already explained, as long as they are capped there is no danger of "effort rating inflation." But how should average caps be set?

If one believes that among workplaces with large numbers of people differences in average efforts cannot be significant, then the average effort rating for all worker councils should be the same. However, if there are many worker councils with few members so the law of large numbers does not apply, and/or one believes there may be significant differences in effort, on average, even among large workplaces, this would be unfair to workers in councils who do work harder on average. An obvious alternative is to cap average effort ratings at 100 times the social benefit to cost ratio for each enterprise. For example, a worker council with a social benefit to cost ratio of 1.01 would have its average effort rating capped at 101, while a worker council with a social benefit to cost ratio of 1.15 would have its average effort rating capped at 115. This would be fair if we believe the participatory planning process estimates social costs and benefits accurately. Because if it does, then any differences in the quality of resources, machinery, produced inputs, or skills of workers will already be reflected in differences in estimates of the opportunity and social costs of the inputs they work with, and therefore any differences in social benefit to cost ratios must be due to differences in effort. However, if we don't think the process of estimating opportunity and social costs is accurate enough to fully "level the playing field" among worker councils, this procedure for setting caps risks being unfair to councils with inputs whose lower quality is not fully reflected in lower estimates of their opportunity or social costs. Which procedure for capping average effort ratings in worker councils is something that will have to be discussed and debated by people in real world participatory economies to be decided as they see fit.

CHAPTER SIXTEEN
INVESTMENT AND DEVELOPMENT PLANNING

When we talk about comprehensive, national, economic planning, this actually includes three different kinds of planning: annual planning, investment planning, and long-run development planning. In the earlier chapter on participatory planning, without being explicit I was talking about annual planning, and explaining why participatory annual planning was preferable not only to coordination through markets and central planning by an elite, but to other conceptions of annual democratic planning as well.

At a theoretical level the only difference between annual, investment, and development planning is the length of time involved. Moreover, what we want to accomplish is the same in all three cases: We want people to have input over decisions to the degree they are affected. We want outcomes to be fair and efficient. We want procedures to promote rather than undermine solidarity. We want all our plans to be environmentally sustainable. Therefore, since we have already discovered that the participatory planning procedure presented earlier best aids us in all these goals, we should try to organize investment and development planning along similar lines. However, when we leave the fantasy world of one planning process planning for all time with complete certainty, and enter the real world where we must engage in separate annual, investment, and development planning processes, difficulties arise we did not have to deal with in annual planning.

Additional Complications

Some problems are obvious: Uncertainty increases the farther in the future we try to calculate. People's preferences and productive technologies change over time. Many who we are planning for have yet to be born, and therefore cannot participate in making decisions that will affect them greatly. If these were not enough problems, there is an additional problem that is less obvious to casual observers: opportunity costs, and the social costs that depend on them, will vary depending on what investment and development plans we choose, which means we may misevaluate investment and development options using today's opportunity and social costs.

To all intents and purposes productive resources, capital stocks, and consumer preferences are all fixed when we formulate annual plans. That is why opportunity and social costs can be estimated with some degree of accuracy through an iterative process of self-activity proposals, provided planning procedures are properly designed to do so. But opportunity costs, and therefore social costs of production in future years as well, will vary to some extent depending on what investments we choose to make this year. And both will vary even more depending on what long-run development trajectory we choose. This means that evaluating different investment and development plans using the estimates of opportunity and social costs derived from this year's participatory annual planning process can be misleading.[1]

When we engage in three distinct planning processes, we introduce a troubling circularity into investment and develop-

---

1   This is not a problem unique to participatory planning. Authoritarian planning and market systems face the same dilemma but in effect, simply pretend the problem does not exist. Nobody knows what future costs and prices will be. So people look at present costs and prices, and make adjustments using more or less complicated forecasting methodologies. But in the end these are simply more or less accurate guesses.

ment planning. Just as opportunity and social costs are the key information needed to know how best to use fixed amounts of different productive resources in our annual production plan, the social rate of return on investment expanding different stocks, or increasing capacity in different industries, is the key information needed for investment planning. The whole purpose of investment planning is to decide how we want to change those stocks and capacities. How much do we want to increase the capacity of the solar industry and decrease the capacity of the coal industry? Is it more important to increase the stock of drill presses or lathes? Should we train more carpenters or more welders? Investment planning is about changing the stocks of different kinds of natural, produced, and human "capital." Investment should go to increasing whatever productive stocks, and the capacities of whatever industries, have the highest social rate of return. But depending on how much we decide to expand the stock of lathes, the opportunity cost of using lathes in the future will be different, and the social cost of producing goods with lathes in the future will therefore be different as well. Future opportunity costs cannot be calculated without knowing how much different productive stocks have been expanded by our investment plan. But we cannot calculate the social rate of return on different investment options without knowing what those future opportunity and social costs will be.

In one sense the results from longer-term planning make shorter-term planning easier because they provide us with some important decisions that have already been made. For example, when doing annual planning we don't have to worry about how much the solar panel and wind turbine industries should each expand this year since that has already been decided by the investment plan covering this year. But unfortunately results from shorter-term planning fail to provide what would most help us when we do longer-term planning. Opportunity costs of productive stocks generated by this year's annual planning procedure are not necessarily reliable estimates of what the future opportunity costs of those productive stocks will be, and it is those future opportunity costs we need to calculate future social costs of producing goods and services, and it is those future social costs we need to calculate social rates of return on investments to engage in sensible investment planning.

Investment Planning

Besides the obvious implication—estimates of social rates of return we use when we do investment planning will be less accurate than estimates of opportunity and social costs we use in annual planning—what other problems will predictably plague investment planning?

First, since estimates of social rates of return on investment options are less reliable than estimates of opportunity and social costs this year, there will be more to dispute and argue over when we engage in investment and development planning. During annual planning, if a worker council wants to claim it is using productive resources efficiently even though its social benefit to cost ratio is lower than average, it must argue that some benefit or cost has been neglected in the analysis (most probably because it cannot be easily quantified) and were this neglected effect considered, it would tip the balance in its favor. To claim that an opportunity cost used in the calculation is grossly inaccurate is unlikely to be compelling. But during the investment planning process, if the solar power industry federation wants to claim that it deserves more investment resources, it can argue on two fronts. It can claim there are considerations that were not taken into account when the social rate of return on investment in the solar industry was calculated; again, most likely because they are difficult to quantify. But it can also claim that using today's opportunity and social costs when calculating social rates of return on investment is misleading, and that a plausible adjustment to what those costs will become in the future under a particular investment plan would yield a higher estimate of the social rate of return on solar power.

The second problem is that the most important participants in development and investment planning will be industry and consumer *federations*, rather than individual worker and consumer councils. Since those who deliberate in federations are *delegates* who represent their fellow workers and consumers, this means that deliberations over investment and development planning will be more representative and less direct than deliberations over annual planning. The deliberations of delegates over investment and development plans can, and should be guided not only by constant consultation between delegates and those they represent, but also by straw polls and preliminary referenda among federation members. Final decisions about investment and development plans can, and should, be settled by referenda, not votes by delegates. But while "self-proposals" by industry and consumer federations can still play an important role in investment and development planning, lacking an accurate way to calculate estimates of social rates of return for different investment "self-proposals" to compare them quantitatively leaves a greater role for discussion and debate among representatives from different federations at national investment planning meetings. It also means that efficient comprehensive investment plans cannot be easily produced by a procedure that modifies "self-proposals" into comprehensive plans in the same way that efficient comprehensive annual plans can be formulated. All of this means there is a greater role for comprehensive proposals whose merits must then be debated by delegates when we engage in investment planning than when we engage in participatory annual planning.

Development Planning

Long-term, structural, or development planning is just investment planning over a longer time frame, which magnifies the problems just discussed. In what order, and how fast should we replace fossil fuels with renewables, weatherize ex-

isting buildings, make new buildings conform to Leeds certifi-
cation standards, rebuild the electric grid, eliminate pesticides
and chemical fertilizers from agriculture, replace cars with
buses, trolleys, subways, or bikes? Or, should we instead prioritize redesigning neighborhoods so more people can walk to
work, school, stores, and entertainment? Unfortunately, just as
estimates of social rates of return on investments in different
sectors are less accurate than estimates of the opportunity and
social costs that emerge from the annual planning process, and
depend on those estimates, estimates of the social rate of return
on alternative structural transformations are less accurate than
estimates of social rates of return on specific investment projects, and depend on those estimates. This implies that during
development planning even more of the discussion and decision making process will be based on qualitative arguments and
opinions that cannot be as convincingly backed by quantitative
estimates alone, and representatives from federations participating in long-run development planning will have to deliberate with even less guidance.

Conclusions

This chapter has forthrightly highlighted difficulties that
will arise when people attempt to tackle investment and development planning in participatory and democratic ways.
The most important danger to bear in mind is that it will predictably be more difficult to stimulate popular participation
on the part of ordinary workers and consumers in investment
and development planning than in annual planning. This is
not only because investment and development decisions affect
their lives today less than decisions made during annual planning. It is also because (1) representatives will play a greater
role in investment and development planning, even if a short
list of alternative investment and development plans delegates
formulate are subject to popular referenda, and (2) "self-proposals," which hold greater interest for most people, will play
a smaller role in investment and development planning than

in annual planning.

Therefore, it is all the more important to maximize popular participation of ordinary workers and consumers during the annual planning process by using the participatory planning procedure. Participatory annual planning is a powerful school teaching ordinary people how their wishes are related to the desires and circumstances of others, and how to coordinate their interrelated activities fairly and efficiently. Annual planning through direct democracy is also the most effective way to counter the danger of a planning elite emerging from among delegates sent off to deliberate over investment and development plans.

CHAPTER SEVENTEEN

PROTECTING THE ENVIRONMENT

Our present economies are not just environmentally un-sustainable, they are crashing vital ecosystems at breakneck speed. Absent a massive *Green New Deal* that replaces fossil fuels with renewable energy sources and dramatically increases energy efficiency in agriculture, industry, transportation, and all parts of the built environment within the next several decades, we are at risk of behaving like the proverbial lemmings. The question we should ask regarding any economic system is whether or not its basic economic institutions afford creative ideas and proposals about how we relate to the natural environment a fair and friendly hearing. The profit motive ignores many environmental effects unmeasured in the commercial nexus. Markets are biased in favor of economic activities that pollute and against activities that preserve and restore valuable ecosystems. Capitalism promotes private consumption over social consumption, and leisure to the detriment of the environment as well. In other words, capitalism is incapable of granting ideas about how to better relate to the natural environment a fair hearing. The question here is whether or not the basic institutions of a participatory economy—democratic worker and consumer councils and federations, remuneration according to effort and need, jobs balanced for empowerment and desirability, and participatory planning— create an institutional setting and incentives that promote judicious relations with our natural environment. When ideas like organic farming, recycling, locally grown produce, smart growth, de-automobilization, energy conservation, increasing energy efficiency, solar and wind power, and more leisure are proposed in a participatory economy, will we discover they must swim against the current, as they do in capitalist economies, or will they find the stream is at long last flowing in their direction?

Protecting the Environment in Annual Plans

As long as producers and consumers are not forced to bear the costs of pollution resulting from their decisions, we will continue to pollute too much. How does participatory planning internalize the negative external effects of pollution? In each iteration in the annual planning procedure there is an "indicative price" for every pollutant in every region impacted representing the current estimate of the damage, or social cost of releasing a unit of that pollutant into the region. What is a pollutant and what is not is decided by federations representing those who live in a region, who are advised by scientists employed in R&D operations run by their federation. For example, if only the residents of ward 2 of Washington, D.C. feel they are adversely affected by a pollutant released in ward 2, then ward 2 is the relevant region. But if the federation representing residents of all wards of Washington, D.C. decides that residents of all wards are affected by a pollutant released in ward 2, then the entire city of Washington is the relevant region. Whereas, if the federation representing all who live in the Chesapeake Bay watershed feels that all who live in the watershed are adversely impacted by a pollutant released in ward 2, then the relevant region includes the District of Columbia, Maryland, and parts of Virginia, Delaware, Pennsylvania and New York State.

If a worker council proposes to emit x units of a particular pollutant into an affected region they are "charged" the indicative price for releasing that pollutant in the region times x, just as they are charged y times the indicative price of a ton of steel if they propose to use y tons of steel as inputs in their production process, and just as they are charged z times the indicative price of an hour of welding labor if they propose to use z hours of welding labor. In other words, any pollutants the worker council proposes to emit is counted as part of the social cost of its proposal, just as the cost of making the steel and the opportunity cost of the welding labor they propose to use are counted as part of the social cost of its proposal—all to be weighed against the social benefits of the outputs they propose to make.

The consumer federation for the region affected looks at the indicative price for a unit of any pollutant that impacts the region and decides how many units it wishes to allow to be emitted. *The federation can decide they do not wish to permit any units of a pollutant to be emitted, in which case no worker council operating in the region will be allowed to emit any of that pollutant. But, if the federation decides to allow X units of a pollutant to be emitted in the region, then the regional federation is "credited" with X times the indicative price for that pollutant.*

What does it mean for a consumer federation to be "credited?" It means the federation will be permitted to buy more public goods for its members to consume than would otherwise be possible given the effort ratings of its members. Or, it means the members of the federation will be able to consume more individually than their effort ratings from work would otherwise warrant. In other words, residents of a region have a right not to be polluted if they so choose. On the other hand, if they choose to tolerate a certain amount of pollution they are compensated for the damage they choose to endure.

This procedure allows people in different regions to choose different tradeoffs between less pollution and more consumption. Why should we want to do this? Citizens in different communities might have different opinions about how damaging pollution is, or how beneficial consumption is. Or, even if all effects could be estimated with certainty, not all people may feel the same about how much they value environmental preservation versus consumption, and citizens in different regions may feel differently on average as well. Does this create the kind of "race to the bottom effect" environmentalists point out that local, as opposed to national standards, do today?[1]

First of all, and most importantly, we are *not* talking about allowing localities to make decisions about pollution that also affects people residing in different localities. We are *not* talking about what are called "spillover effects." For example the ward 2 council will not be permitted to decide how much of a pollutant can be emitted in the ward if the emission damages people living in other wards, or an entire watershed, as well. The spillover problem is solved by the rule that emissions are governed during the planning procedure by federations that include *all* those in the region affected. Instead, the question here is whether or not there is reason to fear a race to be bottom effect if standards for truly local pollutants are left to localities rather than set by higher level authorities.

It is important to remember that in a participatory economy there are no significant differences in income and wealth among communities. For this reason permitting communities to choose their own environmental standards does not risk creating a "race to the bottom effect" in a participatory economy. It certainly does in a society where poor communities are unfairly tempted to permit greater environmental destruction to attract jobs and income while only wealthy communities can afford the luxury of strict pollution controls.

However, the above procedure in the annual planning

---

1   Among those who argue persuasively that local standards under capitalism create an unfortunate "race to the bottom effect" are Kristen H. Engel, "State Environmental Standard Setting: Is There a 'Race to the Bottom'?" *Hasting Law Journal 48*, no. 2, 1997, and Barry G. Rabe, "Power to the States: The Promise and Pitfalls of Decentralization" in *Environmental Policy in the 1990s: Reform or Reaction*, 2nd edition, Norman Vig and Michael Kraft editors, Washington DC Congressional Quarterly Press, 1997.

process protects the environment sufficiently only if present residents in the region of impact are the only ones who suffer adverse consequences. While this is the case for some pollutants such as certain kinds of airborne particulate matter whose effects are confined to a metropolitan area and dissipate quickly, it is often the case that adverse effects of pollution persist over long periods of time so that future generations bear a great deal of the cost of pollution today. The interests of future generations must be protected in the long-run participatory planning process and by an active environmental movement, as explained below. However, before moving on to the long-run planning process and other features of a participatory economy that help protect the environment, it is worth noting how much of an improvement the annual participatory planning process provides over market systems. Under traditional assumptions the above procedure will: (1) reduce pollution to "efficient" levels, (2) satisfy the "polluter pays principle," (3) compensate the actual victims of pollution for the damage they suffer, and (4) induce councils and federations of "affected parties" to truthfully reveal the extent to which they are damaged by pollution. In other words, the procedure is what economists call "incentive compatible."

When producers or consumers have incentives to ignore damaging effects of their choices on the environment, the economic system is marred by perverse incentives. When pollution victims lack incentives to reveal how much they are truly damaged by pollution, the system is not incentive compatible. But in a participatory economy since producers are charged for harmful emissions, the damage from pollution is included in the cost of a worker council proposal, giving producers just as much incentive to reduce pollution as any other cost of production. Since the indicative prices consumers are charged for goods in participatory planning include the costs of pollution associated with their consumption, there is just as much incentive for consumers to reduce consumption of goods that cause pollution as there is for them to reduce consumption of goods that require scarce productive resources or unpleasant labor to produce.

But does the procedure yield an accurate estimate of the damage, or social cost of emissions? In most cases it is reasonable to assume that as emission levels increase, the costs to victims of additional pollution rise, and the benefits to producers and consumers of permitting additional pollution fall. In which case the efficient level of pollution is the level at which the cost of the last unit emitted is equal to the benefit from the last unit emitted. What will happen if the IFB quotes a price for a pollutant less than the "efficient" price, i.e. less than the price at which the last unit of emissions causes damage equal to its benefits? In this case the pollution victims, represented by their federation, will not find it in their interest to permit as much pollution as polluters would like (i.e. there will be excess demand for permission to pollute) and the IFB will increase the indicative price for the pollutant in the next round of planning. If the IFB quotes a price higher than the efficient price, the federation representing pollution victims will offer to permit more pollution than polluters will ask to emit (i.e. there will be an excess supply of permission to pollute) and the IFB will decrease the indicative price in the next round. As long as polluters and federations representing affected parties treat the "price quotes" from the IFB as givens, as they are directed to do, this process will yield the optimal level of pollution.

Uncorrected markets accomplish none of the four goals above. In theory, if all markets were corrected by pollution taxes set equal to the magnitude of the damage caused a market system could achieve efficient levels of pollution.[2] However, *markets provide no signals to help us know how high pollution taxes should be.* On the other hand, a participatory economy not only awards victims an incontestable right *not* to be polluted, it generates an accurate quantitative estimate of

---

2   Economists call these "Pigovian" taxes in honor of A.C. Pigou who first pointed out that such taxes are necessary to correct for inefficiencies caused by externalities in market economies.

how high the indicative price charged for polluting should be.

Protecting the Environment in Long-Run Plans

The fact that annual participatory planning can treat pollution and environmental preservation in an "incentive compatible" way is a major accomplishment and significant improvement over market economies. But while annual participatory planning may "settle accounts" efficiently and equitably concerning the environment for all those taking part in the various councils and federations, what protects the interests of future generations who cannot speak for themselves? How can we avoid intergenerational inequities and inefficiencies while preserving economic democracy when much of the adverse effects of environmental deterioration will fall on the unborn, who obviously cannot be part of democratic decision making processes today?

The interests of future generations, which include the future state of the natural environment, must always be protected, or ignored, by the present generation. This is true whether it is a political or economic elite in the present generation that weighs the interests of the present generation against those of future generations, or a democratic decision making process involving all members of the present generation. In a participatory economy, intergenerational efficiency and equity regarding the environment must be achieved in the same way intergenerational efficiency and equity is achieved in all other regards: by means of restraints the present generation places on itself in its democratic deliberations concerning long-run plans.

If the long-run plan calls for more overall investment, this decreases the amount of consumption available to the present generation in this year's annual plan. If the long-run plan calls for reducing the automobile fleet and expanding rail service in the future, this reduces the amount of investment and productive resources this year's annual plan is permitted to allocate to worker councils making automobiles, and increases the amount of investment and resources to be allocated to worker councils making trains. If the long-run plan calls for a 25% reduction in national carbon emissions over five years, the national consumer federation must reduce the amount of carbon emissions it permits in each of the next five annual plans accordingly. Major changes in the energy, transportation, and housing sectors, as well as conversions from polluting to "green" technologies and products, are all determined by the long-run planning process where it is as easy for federations to express preferences for investments in environmental protection and restoration as for investments that permit future increases in private consumption.

There is no way to guarantee that members of the present generation will take the interests of future generations sufficiently to heart, or, for that matter, choose wisely for them even when there is no intergenerational conflict of interest. Whether or not the present generation decides on a long-run plan democratically or autocratically, there is no way to guarantee it will not make mistakes that damage future generations. Maybe replacing cars with trains for our descendants is a mistake because solar powered cars will prove to be as environmentally friendly as trains and more convenient. Nor is there any way to make sure the present generation will not behave like Louis XV and simply decide, *Après moi, le déluge.* We can hope that people who practice economic justice diligently among themselves, as a participatory economy requires, will practice it on behalf of their children, grandchildren, and great grandchildren as well. We can hope that people used to permitting pollution only when the benefits outweigh the costs will apply the same principle in their long-run planning and include the costs to those they know will follow them. We can hope that when people have choices posed in ways that make perfectly clear when they would be favoring themselves unfairly at the expense of their descendants, that they will be too ashamed to do so.

Long-run participatory planning is designed to make issues of intergenerational equity and efficiency as clear as possible. Annual participatory planning is designed to estimate the detrimental and beneficial effects of economic choices on the environment accurately and incorporate them into the overall costs and benefits that must be weighed. But even so, there is no guarantee that future generations and the environment might not be slighted. Some, like Dr. Seuss' Lorax, will have to speak up in the long-run participatory planning process when they think others in their generation are neglecting future generations and the environment.

Other Environmental Protections

Besides specific features of the annual and long-run planning processes discussed above, there are other features of a participatory economy that make it more likely people will treat the natural environment judiciously. (1) An egalitarian distribution of wealth and income means nobody will be so poor and desperate that they cannot afford to prioritize environmental preservation over material consumption. There will be no destitute colonists cutting down and burning valuable rain forests because they have no other way to stay alive. There will be no poverty stricken local communities who acquiesce to host unsafe toxic waste dumps because they are desperate for jobs and income. An egalitarian distribution of income and wealth also means nobody will be so rich they can buy private environmental amenities while leaving the public environment to deteriorate. (2) A system that minimizes the use of material incentives and emphasizes rewards for social serviceability greatly diminishes the environmentally destructive effects of conspicuous consumption. There is ample evidence that what Juliet Schor calls "competitive consumption"[3] drives many to consume far beyond the point where additional consumption generates more wellbeing than the cost of leisure

3 Juliet Schor, *The Overspent American*, New York: Basic Books, 1998.

lost. There is good reason to believe this phenomenon will die out in a participatory economy. (3) An allocative system that provides productive resources to workers as long as the social benefits of their work exceed the social costs (including the environmental costs) eliminates the competitive rat race for producers to accumulate and grow despite adverse environmental consequences. In other words, unlike capitalist economies, there is no unhealthy and environmentally destructive "growth imperative" in a participatory economy.

However, in the end there is nothing a democratic economy can do to prevent environmental abuse if people make unwise or selfish choices. This can happen because people are simply unaware of the detrimental environmental consequences of their choices, or underestimate their severity. This can occur because the present generation is selfish and cares more about itself than about future generations. Or, if one believes that other species have rights or interests that deserve to be taken into account, it can be because people refuse to do so. An active environmental movement educating and agitating for its causes will be necessary in a participatory economy, and the health of the biosphere will depend on this movement's wisdom, strength and persuasive powers. The difference is that in a participatory economy environmentalists will find favorable settings for presenting their case, whereas in capitalism the deck is heavily stacked against them.

CHAPTER EIGHTEEN

FROM HERE TO THERE

Only a few years ago it was difficult to imagine how we could move from a world celebrating the economics of competition and greed as never before to a world practicing the economics of equitable cooperation. With the exception of a few Latin American countries who had turned away from neoliberalism to search for a new and different "twenty-first century socialism," there was little reason to be optimistic. But that was before the financial crisis of 2008. That was before the Great Recession engulfed the advanced economies in Europe and North America. That was before median family wealth in the US dropped back to its level in 1990, "erasing two decades of accumulated prosperity" in the words of the Federal Reserve Bank. That was before the unemployment rate in the eurozone hit an all time high in March 2012. That was before the unemployment rates in Spain and Greece surged past 20%, and over 50% for Spanish and Greek youth. In other words, that was before capitalism reminded us once again just how inhumane, unfair, and wasteful of economic potentials it can be.

That was also before demonstrations against corruption and police violence shook Greece, and voters in Iceland refused to pay to bailout creditors of Icelandic banks in 2009. That was before student strikes led to the rise of the Uncut movement in the UK in the fall of 2010. That was before long silenced popular forces rose up in the astonishing "Arab

Spring," and before the rise of the "indignados" in Spain in the spring of 2011. That was before the electorate showed right center and left center governments administering inhumane and futile economic austerity policies the door in every country in the eurozone. That was before the people of Wisconsin occupied their state house in the winter of 2011 in protest against austerity and union busting. That was before the incredible Occupy Wall Street movement spread to thousands of cities and towns across the United States in the fall of 2011. That was before students rebelled in Quebec in the spring of 2012. That was before the wheels came off the neoliberal austerity wagon in Greece when a radical left party came within an eye-lash of winning a national election on June 17, 2012, and being able to form a left government pledged to repudiate unpayable debt, nationalize the banks, end inhumane and futile austerity, and pursue an altogether different economic model. In other words, that was before hundreds of millions of people began to say: "ENOUGH! We can, and will do better than ruling elites, whom we will no longer tolerate."

Halfway through 2012 the prospects for system change look very different than they did only four years ago. We are still a long way from replacing the economics of competition and greed with the economics of equitable cooperation. But at least it is easier to see what the way forward looks like. Those of us who want to see economic "system change" need to make even more progress in five areas.

(1) We need to build bigger and stronger economic reform movements. Old reform movements like the labor, consumer, and anti-corporate movements must be revitalized. New movements like Uncut, Occupy, and "los indignados" led by a new generation of activists, pioneering new strategies and tactics, must grow bigger and stronger. Otherwise we will never build majoritarian support for social change. But we need more than stronger economic movements. Without strong social movements for civil, racial, women, and gay rights, without a strong peace movement, and without a strong environ-

mental movement, stronger economic reform movements will not suffice to put the economics of competition and greed behind us. To make a long story short, the nasty habits we must put behind us form a mutually reinforcing package that must be replaced by a new set of institutions and behaviors in all spheres of social life.

We also need to understand that people have every right to expect those who want system change to be completely dedicated to making reform campaigns as successful as possible, and every right to consider us AWOL if we do not. But this does not mean we must allow others in reform movements to limit what we, who also want system change, have to say. We *do* know something most others in various reform movements at this point do not: that capitalism must eventually be replaced altogether with a system of equitable cooperation—and we should always insist on our right to explain why to those we work with.

When we work in the labor movement we must teach not only that profit income is unfair, but that the salaries of highly paid professionals are also unfair when they are paid many times more than ordinary workers while making fewer personal sacrifices. We must be clear that workers in less developed countries deserve incomes commensurate with their efforts, just as workers in the United States and Europe do. In other words, when we work in the labor movement we must insist that the labor movement live up to its billing and become an uncompromising hammer for justice. When we work in the consumer movement, even while we campaign against price gouging and defective products, we must also make clear how the market system inefficiently promotes excessive individual consumption at the expense of social consumption and leisure. When we work in the anti-corporate movement we must never tire of emphasizing that corporations and their unprecedented power are the major problem in the world today. We must make clear that every concession corporations make is because it is rung out of them by activists who convince them that the anti-corporate movement will inflict greater losses on their bottom line if they persist in their anti-social and environmentally destructive behavior than if they accede to our demands. When we participate in campaigns to fully fund public education and cancel unpayable student debt we must make clear that just because someone is more educated than someone else is no reason they should enjoy a higher standard of living than people who work just as hard as they do. When we promote policies like pollution taxes to modify incentives for private corporations in the market system, we must also make clear that production for profit and market forces are the worst enemies of the environment, and that the environment will never be adequately protected until those economic institutions are replaced. Working wholeheartedly in reform campaigns and movements does *not* mean we must adopt reformist politics, which we know will fail to achieve equitable cooperation in the twenty-first century, just as it did in the twentieth century.

(2) We need to create more experiments in participatory, equitable cooperation, allowing more people to treat one another in ways that "prefigure" the new society. Without palpable proof that participatory, equitable cooperation is not only possible, but works better than competition and greed for people who embrace it, we will never convince people to support fundamental system change. We need to create more worker and consumer owned cooperatives. When private owners want to shut down factories leaving employees and communities destitute we need to organize campaigns for workers to take them over with community backing. We need to turn community development corporations into real vehicles for achieving community economic development: prioritizing job creation for disadvantaged residents rather than more privileged outsiders, prioritizing renovation and affordable housing rather than gentrification, and empowering civic organizations rather than local king-pins. We need to launch more campaigns for participatory budgeting where neighborhood assemblies decide democratically how they want to spend their taxes. We need to create more egalitarian and sustainable living commu-

nities in cities as well as rural areas for those ready and able to live according to our new values.

Work to reform capitalism and work to create experiments in equitable cooperation are both necessary but neither strategy is effective by itself. Only in combination do they protect us from the predictable pit falls of each approach. Reforms alone cannot achieve equitable cooperation because as long as the institutions of private enterprise and markets are left in place to reinforce anti-social behavior based on greed and fear, progress toward equitable cooperation will be limited, and the danger of retrogression will be ever present. On the other hand, concentrating exclusively on organizing alternative economic institutions within capitalist economies also cannot be successful because it isolates us from too many who cannot become involved, and because market forces constantly pressure alternative institutions to abandon cooperative principles to ensure commercial success. Fortunately, working on reform campaigns helps overcome the danger of isolation inherent in building prefigurative projects, while continuing to improve our understanding of how equitable cooperation can work helps prevent those working for reform from giving up on "system change" and "settling" for a slightly improved system still based on competition and greed.

(3) The US left needs an electoral strategy. We cannot simply turn up our noses at "traditional politics" and stand aloof from electoral campaigns. We can complain about it, but the fact is a high percentage of people we must mobilize pay attention to politics primarily during election season. Abandoning the field whenever people come out to play the game is hardly a strategy for winning! Nor can we forever participate in elections only by running "protest" candidates who seek to expose the hypocrisy of traditional political parties and raise issues mainstream candidates and media avoid, but who have no chance of winning. Candidates with no chance of winning command too little attention not only from the media but from the public as well.

I am not suggesting we subordinate other areas of left activism to focus more on electing officials who sing a progressive tune during election season only to betray progressives who campaigned and voted for them once in office. Unfortunately, far from being the "beacon of democracy" tinhorn patriots proclaim, the US Constitution—and a Supreme Court which abuses its power to "interpret" the Constitution to promote a conservative agenda—have become strait jackets preventing the popular will from manifesting itself through elections. At this point the odds against electing progressive politicians and holding them accountable to their campaign rhetoric in the US are becoming prohibitive. We live in a two party duopoly where both parties are increasingly beholden to corporations and wealthy donors. So progressives who prioritize electoral work in the US must first and foremost wage major campaigns to win campaign finance reform and proportional representation before there is any hope of imitating the kind of success left political parties like Syriza had recently in Greece. This is a monumental, but necessary task. Since we in the US will eventually need to build our own Syriza, we must come up with a successful strategy to fix an electoral system that is now rigged to make this impossible.

(4) We will also need a strategy to defend popular victories from anti-democratic forces. There is no reason to believe ruling elites will abide by the results of fair elections, or shrink from destroying activist organizations and alternative experiments that challenge their ideology, power, and privilege. We must not only have a strategy to build, but a strategy to defend what we build as well. The age of revolutionaries picking up the gun is over. If twenty-first century politics gives way to warfare we will lose. Therefore, our defense strategy (and we will need one) must be centered on organizing for massive resistance and non-compliance since no elite, no matter how well armed, can rule unless we, the people, carry out their orders.

(5) Finally, we need to become more clear and concrete about just how we propose economic decisions be made dif-

ferently. The first attempts at post-capitalist economies (twentieth century Communism) had little to recommend them, and people have every right to be skeptical and demand that those calling for system change be very clear about how the new system would go about organizing economic decision making differently. The purpose of this short book is to increase the quality of discussion about how we can best organize an economics of equitable cooperation.

It is important to understand that while all these activities are necessary for success, (a) not everyone must participate in every necessary activity, (b) the most productive mixture will be different in different places and times, and (c) political groups with different ideologies will prioritize one form of activity over another. But since we need to make a great deal of progress in all five areas there is little need to waste time now squabbling over which area is most strategic.

A Green New Deal

One of the great mass movements of the early twenty-first century must be a movement to secure a *Green New Deal*. Scientists warn us that unless global greenhouse gas emissions are reduced by at least 80% before mid-century we run an unacceptable risk of triggering irreversible, cataclysmic climate change. Yet emissions continue to rise while international negotiations and domestic climate policy go nowhere. The bad news is that the financial and economic crisis has distracted attention from the looming crisis of climate change. The good news is there is a single solution to both the economic and ecological crises—a Green New Deal.

Replacing fossil fuels with renewables, transforming not only transportation but industry and agriculture as well to be much more energy efficient, and rebuilding our entire built environment to conserve energy will be an immense, historic undertaking. What is needed if we are to avoid unacceptable climate change is the greatest technological "reboot" in economic history.

It is now four years since the financial crisis catapulted us into the Great Recession, with unemployment rates on the rise again in Europe and the United States with no end in sight. As I write one out of six American workers is still unemployed or underemployed, and the situation in Europe is far worse.

If we do not put hundreds of millions of people to work over the next few decades in Europe and North America transforming *Fossil-fuel-estan* into *Renew-conserve-estan* we will literally broil ourselves to death at some point in the century ahead. If we fail to create hundreds of millions of new jobs turning *Fossil-fuel-estan* into *Renew-conserve-estan* the Great Recession will persist indefinitely and the young generation in Europe and North America will face a jobless future. Two problems. One solution. A massive Green New Deal.

As Van Jones, soon to be appointed special advisor to the President for green jobs, put it in 2008: "The generations living today get to retrofit, reboot, and reenergize a nation. We get to rescue and reinvent the US economy. The more aggressive we are, the better off we will be. There is a better future out there." Unfortunately Van Jones was dismissed by President Obama under pressure from conservatives after being on the job for less than six months. Much that progressive activists do over the next decade will revolve around building a domestic political coalition powerful enough to launch a massive Green New Deal.

Notice how the "growth vs. the environment" trade off disappears in a Green New Deal. Whenever economic growth slows, the labor movement, quite understandably, clamors for more economic stimulus to put people back to work. But whenever the economy grows more rapidly, the environmental movement complains, also understandably, that more production puts more strain on the environment and is unsustainable. *But it depends on what we are producing!*

If we are building more McMansions for the 1%, putting more cars in every garage, paving more roads and highways, and building new port terminals to ship more coal to Asia then getting jobs by increasing production does put unsustainable pressure on the environment. But if we create more jobs for laid off construction workers retrofitting buildings and houses so they will be more energy efficient; if we re-build and expand public transportation systems; if we create more teaching jobs to train the new generation to transform and operate a decentralized electric grid that welcomes electricity from hundreds of millions of rooftops and substitutes local sources for distant central generators wherever possible; if we put laid off coal miners to work assembling wind turbines and installing solar panels on roof tops... then the new jobs are producing things we desperately need to save the environment, not what ecological economists call "through-put" intensive consumption goods that destroy the environment.

In sum, only a Green New Deal can provide people what they cannot find now, and want more than anything else: socially useful work. And only a Green New Deal will prevent climate change that unleashes unthinkable destruction.

New Beginnings

There are so many new beginnings scattered around the world it would be impossible to list even a fraction. The two described briefly below are only examples of places where the kind of multipart strategy outlined above is already in motion.

Greece: Activists in Greece have arguably made more progress in all five areas described above than anywhere else in Europe or North America.

The economic crisis hit sooner and harder in Greece, where unions and organizations supporting social services were also stronger initially. The rebellion against police brutality and corruption led by young anti-authoritarians in 2009 placed important constraints on repressive forces. The mass movement opposing inhumane and pointless fiscal austerity demanded by the "troika" (the European Commission, the European Central Bank, and the International Monetary Fund) negotiated and administered first by the New Democracy-led center right government, and after 2009 by the Pasok-led center left government, has been more powerful in Greece than anywhere else. In large part the success of anti-austerity forces in Greece stems from the ability of traditional progressive organizations, representing older generations, and new anti-authoritarian organizations, representing young people, to work effectively together.

As the "official" Greek economy has shrunk, leaving more and more people unable to meet their basic economic needs, young anti-authoritarian groups have built a strong, environmentally conscious, "solidarity" economy. Whole neighborhoods in Athens now function largely outside the capitalist economy. Every summer a massive, two week celebration called the B-fest takes place in Athens where activists and scholars from all over the world join Greeks to discuss what the new world they are building should, and increasingly does look like.

Finally, after it became apparent that Pasok had abandoned all its social democratic principles and become the willing accomplice of neoliberal austerity, a host of small, left political parties finally began to make headway in the electoral arena. The most important grouping known as Syriza rose from less than 5% of the vote in 2009 to over 27% of the vote on June 17, 2012. Support for other left parties rose also as the two traditional parties which had dominated Greek politics for over forty years saw their collective share of the vote shrink from 80% to 33% in less than five years. Had Syriza received 2% more of the vote we would have seen the first radical left government in Europe forthrightly opposing neoliberal capitalism and pioneering a new economic path. Since the New Democracy-Pasok government now in power represents less than 33% of voters, and is committed to administering even more pointless austerity, the day of reckoning in Greece has merely been postponed. But there are signs of new beginnings in the least politically advanced country in the world as well.

Jackson, Mississippi: The purpose of the *Jackson Plan* (www. mxgm.org) is to "apply many of the best practices in the promotion of participatory democracy, solidarity economy, and sustainable development, and combine them with progressive community organizing and electoral politics." Its three fundamental programmatic components are building People's Assemblies, building a network of progressive political candidates, and building a broad based solidarity economy.

Some of its accomplishments to date include electing the first ever Black Sheriff of Hinds County, winning the release of the Scott Sisters (who served sixteen years in jail for *supposedly* robbing a convenience store of $11), saving public transportation in Jackson from devastating austerity cuts, helping defeat Arizona-style anti-immigrant legislation in the state of Mississippi, passing an anti-racial profiling ordinance in Jackson, building a network of mutually supporting worker, housing, and consumer cooperatives, building a network of urban farms, agricultural cooperatives, and farmers markets, and developing community and conservation land trusts.

The Jackson movement has embraced what it calls a "dual power" strategy: "Building autonomous power... in the form of People's Assemblies, and engaging electoral politics on a limited scale with the express intent of building radical voting blocks and electing candidates drawn from the ranks of the Assemblies themselves." And it is working!

Revolution?

Are we talking about a social revolution? Yes, we are. But why should revolutionaries expect revolution to look the same in the twenty-first century as it did in the nineteenth and twentieth centuries? Aren't revolutionaries the ones who foresee changes that others can scarcely imagine? Why should our vision of revolution remain immune from our general expectation that things change?

REFERENCES

- Albert, Michael and Robin Hahnel, *The Political Economy of Participatory Economics* (Princeton University Press, 1991).

- Albert, Michael and Robin Hahnel, "Socialism As It Was Always Meant to Be," *Review of Radical Political Economics (24, 3&4)*, Fall and Winter 1992: 46-66.

- Albert, Michael and Robin Hahnel, "Participatory Planning," *Science & Society (56, 1)*, Spring 1992: 39-59.

- Engel, Kristen, "State Environmental Standard Setting: Is There a 'Race to the Bottom?'" *Hasting Law Journal (48, 2)*, 1997.

- Hahnel, Robin, "Exploitation: A Modern Approach," *Review of Radical Political Economics (38, 2)*, Spring 2006: 175-192.

- Hahnel, Robin, *Green Economics: Confronting the Ecological Crisis* (M.E. Sharpe, 2011).

- Marx, Karl, *Critique of the Gotha Program* (International Publishers, 1938, original publication date 1875).

- Nove, Alec, *The Economics of Feasible Socialism* (George Allen & Unwin, 1983).

- Rabe, Barry, "Power to the States: The Promise and Pitfalls of Decentralization," in *Environmental Policy in the 1990s: Reform or Reaction*, 2nd edition, Norman Vig and Michael Kraft editors, Washington DC Congressional Quarterly Press, 1997.

- Schor, Juliet, *The Overspent American* (Basic Books, 1998).

- Schweickart, David, *Against Capitalism* (Westview Press, 1996).

- Schweickart, David, *After Capitalism* (Rowman & Littlefield, 2002).